T0328782

Cambridge Elements ≡

Elements in Forensic Linguistics
edited by
Tim Grant
Aston University
Tammy Gales
Hofstra University

FORENSIC LINGUISTICS IN AUSTRALIA

Origins, Progress and Prospects

Diana Eades
University of New England

Helen Fraser
University of Melbourne

Georgina Heydon
RMIT University

Shaftesbury Road, Cambridge CB2 8EA, United Kingdom

One Liberty Plaza, 20th Floor, New York, NY 10006, USA

477 Williamstown Road, Port Melbourne, VIC 3207, Australia

314–321, 3rd Floor, Plot 3, Splendor Forum, Jasola District Centre,
New Delhi – 110025, India

103 Penang Road, #05–06/07, Visioncrest Commercial, Singapore 238467

Cambridge University Press is part of Cambridge University Press & Assessment,
a department of the University of Cambridge.

We share the University's mission to contribute to society through the pursuit of
education, learning and research at the highest international levels of excellence.

www.cambridge.org
Information on this title: www.cambridge.org/9781009168106

DOI: 10.1017/9781009168090

First published 2023

A catalogue record for this publication is available from the British Library.

ISBN 978-1-009-16810-6 Paperback
ISSN 2634-7334 (online)
ISSN 2634-7326 (print)

Cambridge University Press & Assessment has no responsibility for the persistence
or accuracy of URLs for external or third-party internet websites referred to in this
publication and does not guarantee that any content on such websites is, or will
remain, accurate or appropriate.

Forensic Linguistics in Australia

Origins, Progress and Prospects

Elements in Forensic Linguistics

DOI: 10.1017/9781009168090
First published online: May 2023

Diana Eades
University of New England

Helen Fraser
University of Melbourne

Georgina Heydon
RMIT University

Author for correspondence: Diana Eades, Diana.Eades@une.edu.au

Abstract: This Element presents an account of forensic linguistics in Australia since the first expert linguistic evidence in 1959, through early work in the 1970s–1980s, the defining of the discipline in the 1990s and into the current era. It starts with a consideration of some widespread misconceptions about language that affect the field and some problematic ideologies in the law, which underlie much of the discussion throughout the Element. The authors' report of forensic linguists' work is structured in terms of the linguistic, interactional and sociocultural contexts of the language data being analysed, whether in expert evidence, in research, or in practical applications of linguistics in a range of legal settings. The Element concludes by highlighting mutual engagement between forensic linguistic practitioners and both the judiciary and legal scholars, and outlines some of the key factors which support a critical forensic linguistics approach in much of the work in the authors' country.

Keywords: language and the law, forensic linguistics, Australian linguistics, applied linguistics, language and justice

ISBNs: 9781009168106 (PB), 9781009168090 (OC)
ISSNs: 2634-7334 (online), 2634-7326 (print)

Contents

Series Preface

The Elements in Forensic Linguistics series from Cambridge University Press publishes across four main topic areas (1) investigative and forensic text analysis; (2) the study of spoken linguistic practices in legal contexts; (3) the linguistic analysis of written legal texts and (4) explorations of the origins, development and scope of the field in various countries and regions. *Forensic Linguistics in Australia: Origins, Progress and Prospects* by Diana Eades, Helen Fraser and Georgina Heydon provides our second Element in this fourth area.

All three authors of *Forensic Linguistics in Australia* have been significant contributors to the discipline. Outside of Australia Diana Eades is perhaps best known for her sociolinguistic work with Indigenous Australians, documenting the linguistic and cultural differences between their societies and the powerful English-speaking societies, and addressing the consequent injustices that have arisen from legal interactions involving the Indigenous peoples. Helen Fraser's work has been in phonetics and phonology with a particular focus on issues of contested transcription of covert audio for use as evidence. Georgina Heydon entered the field of forensic linguistics through her work on the police interview and her attempts to reform interviewing practices across Australia and subsequently extending this work across the global South. All three of their personal academic histories are threads through this Element and we can see how they have contributed to the story of the development of a specifically Australian variety of forensic linguistics. They also bring work of other researchers' topics and insights, demonstrating the maturity of the discipline in Australia and also pointing to the work that still needs to be done.

From my perspective this Element highlights both similarities and differences between Australian and British Forensic Linguistics in terms of the mix of topics and approaches – Australian forensic linguistics is shown to have a very specific flavour. I hope that other readers from the UK and elsewhere round the world will also appreciate both these differences as well as the common endeavour. This is what we hoped for when we had the idea of commissioning the *Origins* subseries and what we look forward to in future Elements.

Our next *Origins* Element will focus on China, and we hope to receive further proposals from any country or region where forensic linguistics is studied or practiced.

Tim Grant
Series Editor

1 Introduction

1.1 Introducing This Element

We are delighted to have this opportunity to present an account of forensic linguistics in Australia. There is a great deal of work to cover, but, mindful of our 'brief' from the series editors, we have necessarily given brief treatment to much of this work. We apologise for having to be selective about citations, not being able to include any theses, and also for any work we have inadvertently overlooked.

Further, we make no attempt to cover the field of forensic linguistics outside Australia. Future Elements from other countries will add to our account of the field in Australia.

In bringing together the work of Australian linguists on language and the law, we write from, and about, several different areas of linguistics. We have attempted some harmonisation of our discussion of diverse sub-disciplinary approaches and of our use of terminology. We hope this will make this publication accessible to scholars and students in linguistics and law, and to law professionals from numerous backgrounds. As the content is necessarily limited in scope, we encourage readers to follow up parts of interest to them with the help of the reference list.

Our Element starts with a short introduction to forensic linguistics, its history in Australia and some of its key features. In Section 2 we introduce some widespread misconceptions about language that affect our field and some problematic language ideologies in the law. We then go on, in Sections 3–5, to report in detail on the work of Australian forensic linguists. Given the central role of context in the workings of language, we have structured these sections in terms of linguistic, interactional and sociocultural contexts of the language data being analysed.

Thus, in Section 3 we deal with linguistic contexts, including, in Sections 3.1–3.5, the areas in which phonetics, phonology, morpho-syntax and semantics are major analytical tools. In Section 3.6 we deal with issues concerning linguistic repertoires, focusing on work involving speakers and signers of languages and dialects other than standard English, and child witnesses. Section 3.7 considers research on laws about language. Section 4 deals with forensic linguistic work that prioritises interactional contextual features and is primarily sociolinguistic. The work reported deals with three main legal settings, namely investigative interviews, courtroom hearings and refugee status determination interviews and related tribunal/courtroom hearings. In all these legal settings interviewing is the central interactional context. In Section 5 we turn to forensic linguistic studies and expert evidence that prioritise the sociocultural context, both of the culture of law and its contrast with other cultural groups and of the impact of sociocultural dimensions of communication. This section draws mainly on sociolinguistic and linguistic anthropological work.

We conclude our Element in Section 6 with a consideration of some of the main features of forensic linguistics in Australia, highlighting both its mutual engagement with practitioners and scholars of law and our understanding of some of the key factors which support a critical forensic linguistics approach in much of the work in our country.

1.2 What Is Forensic Linguistics?

1.2.1 Linguistics

Linguistics is the scientific study of language in general, encompassing scientific study of specific languages (but not mere ability to speak them, nor study of their literature and culture as arts or humanities disciplines) and scientific study of interpreting and translation. Applied linguistics is the use of linguistic knowledge to assist in practical applications. Various branches of linguistics investigate structural, social, cultural, psychological and computational aspects of language and language use. In this Element we use the general term 'linguist' to refer to scholars in any branch of linguistic science, with more specific terms when relevant.

While there is wide variation in the content and orientation of the branches of linguistics, all are based on comprehensive and systematic analysis of empirical evidence, using scientific methods, including observation, hypothesis and analysis.

These methods have enabled linguists to establish an impressive array of scientific findings on a range of topics.

Importantly, many of these findings directly contradict apparent 'facts' about language that are accepted by many people as part of our society's body of 'common knowledge'. A frequent theme in linguistics is that common knowledge about language embodies some misconceptions, sometimes called myths. This creates problems especially for branches of applied linguistics which involve direct interaction between linguists and non-linguists.

1.2.2 Forensic Linguistics

Forensic linguistics is a branch of applied linguistics that uses expertise in linguistics for applications related to legal contexts. Though the origins of the discipline can be traced considerably earlier, the first use of the term 'forensic linguistics' is usually ascribed to Svartvik's (1968) account of his linguistic work on a case in England in which the written record of a police interview included an apparent confession. Svartvik demonstrated that the confession had been fabricated by police – a practice that later came to be known in Australia and the UK as 'verballing' (falsely stating that a suspect had made a verbal admission). Verballing continued as an increasingly serious problem until the introduction of mandatory electronic recording of police interviews with suspects (but see Section 3.1.2).

Since then, forensic linguistics, though still relatively young, has grown to be a well-established interdisciplinary field, with numerous researchers and practitioners around the globe. It has a large literature, several international associations, including, among others, the International Association for Forensic and Legal Linguistics (IAFLL), the International Association for Forensic Phonetics and Acoustics (IAFPA) and a number of journals, including *International Journal of Speech Language and the Law* (IJSLL) and *Language and Law/Linguagem e Direito* (LLLD).

Forensic linguistics can be divided into two interrelated branches, sometimes called 'legal linguistics' and 'forensic linguistics' (this means 'forensic linguistics' is sometimes used as a general term and sometimes more narrowly). Legal linguistics studies how language is used through all stages of the legal process, including court hearings, police and lawyer interviews and many more. While this work has various motivations, one notable theme is a concern to ensure inclusive justice for all, especially for disadvantaged groups, such as Aboriginal people, or those who lack proficiency in spoken or written English.

Forensic linguistics (narrow sense) develops methods for analysing and evaluating language to be used as evidence in courtroom hearings, such as written documents or recorded conversations that provide information relevant to deciding the verdict. Again, this work has multiple motivations, but a notable theme is a concern to ensure justice in the use of language as forensic evidence, despite the widespread misconceptions about language that are embodied in common knowledge.

The present publication aims to give an account of the origins, development and current state of forensic linguistics in Australia from its beginnings in the late 1950s to the present day. While our field is interdisciplinary, we have necessarily restricted the scope of this Element to the work in legal contexts of those trained and qualified in linguistics. A wider focus is beyond the scope of this publication. However, work on language and law by lawyers and interpreters is of great interest and importance to forensic linguists (see Grey & Smith-Khan, 2021).

1.3 Forensic Linguistics in Australia

1.3.1 Precursors 1959–1970s

Linguistic evidence was first presented in an Australian legal matter in 1959, almost a decade before Svartvik coined the term 'forensic linguistics'. The evidence was given by then Reader (later Professor) in Linguistics at Adelaide University, T. G. H. Strehlow, in the South Australian case against Aboriginal man Rupert Max Stuart. Stuart's murder conviction had relied on a confession that Strehlow argued was fabricated, that is that Stuart had been verballed.

Strehlow's expert evidence revealed insights about language variation that were ahead of the field of linguistics in the late 1950s, describing Stuart's way of talking English initially as Pidgin English, and then Northern Territory English, that is, 'the language spoken by most educated part-aboriginals' (note that the term part-aboriginals is no longer acceptable). A decade later, the ground-breaking work of American linguist William Labov on (American) Black English Vernacular resonated with Strehlow's (unpublished) description of Northern Territory English. Central to Labov's work, which revolutionised modern linguistics, was the recognition that the way African Americans speak English is similar to a regional dialect, but it is a dialect whose speakers share ethnicity rather than geography. Although Strehlow used the seemingly geographical term 'Northern Territory English', he defined the variety in terms of the ethnicity of its speakers (see Eades, 2013).

The late Gloria Brennan, a Western Australian woman whose first language was Wongi, was the first Aboriginal person to graduate in linguistics (1978). Her fifty-five-page report (Brennan, 1979) on the need for interpreting and translation services for Aboriginal people was the first linguistic research to deal with language in legal contexts in Australia (commissioned and published by the Australian Government).

With the enactment of land rights for Aboriginal people in the Northern Territory in 1976, many linguists doing research in that jurisdiction became actively involved in the preparation of evidence for land claims. While their work on documenting (often complex) relationships between social groups and language and land has not generally been considered forensic linguistics, the work of Michael Walsh, Harold Koch and a few other linguists on linguistic aspects of this particular legal process is an exception (Sections 3.6.3 and 5).

1.3.2 Early Days (1970s–1980s)

It seems the first branch of linguistics to be commissioned to examine linguistic evidence for its value in identifying the perpetrator of a crime was phonetics. In the infamous Qantas bomb hoax of 1971, telephone messages were recorded in which the caller claimed a plane had been planted with a bomb that would detonate unless a large ransom was paid. Police asked Alex Jones, of Sydney University English Department, for assistance in determining the speaker's accent. The story is taken up in Section 3.2.

From the late 1970s linguists across several additional branches of linguistics were involved in sporadic casework, as documented in Eades (1994). Their work addressed several different legal questions, including speaker identification, degree of pronunciation similarity between two trademarks, disputed transcription of tape-recorded utterances, alleged fabrication of confessional evidence (verballing), authorship attribution, meaning of specific words in Torres Strait Creole and Aboriginal English, and cross-cultural communication issues impacting interviews with an Aboriginal person. However, except for Hammarström (1987), this work was not documented in academic publications, and there was little sense at this stage of forensic linguistics as a unified branch of linguistic science.

Also during the 1980s, Diana Eades was becoming known for her research on the linguistics of Aboriginal English and Aboriginal communication styles. Through this work, she was contacted by defence lawyers concerned about the possible verballing of an Aboriginal client, Kelvin Condren. This resulted in one of her earliest expert linguistic reports, which showed that Condren was highly unlikely to have used language attributed to him in the so-called verbatim transcript of the interview (*R* v. *Condren*, 1987). Eades' report was excluded from the appeal, and Condren remained in prison for several more years, until a journalist's incontrovertible evidence showed he had been in prison at the time of the murder of which he was accused (Section 4.2.1; Eades, 2013).

1.3.3 Defining a Discipline (1990s)

Experience in *Condren* and other cases led Eades to recognise a number of misconceptions and problematic attitudes about language that are embodied in legal practice. For example, lawyers and judges were reluctant to accept Aboriginal English as a rule-governed dialect of English. They saw language as related to biology (e.g. skin colour) rather than socialisation, and they believed linguistic judgments could be made on the basis of common knowledge without need for specialised expertise.

Eades developed a new research programme focused on documenting and countering problematic attitudes and presuppositions in the law, especially as they affected justice for Aboriginal people in the legal process. To bring attention of other linguists to these issues, Eades convened a popular annual workshop on language and the law at the conference of the Australian Linguistics Society (1989–1996). She also collated information about expert linguistic evidence in Australian courts, as well as a growing research base on forensic linguistics, to make it accessible to colleagues (Eades, 1994, 1995).

During these years, Eades became part of a group of linguists around the globe who established forensic linguistics as an international discipline through the International Association of Forensic Linguists (established 1992, renamed the International Association of Forensic and Legal Linguistics in 2021) and the journal *Forensic Linguistics* (established in 1994, renamed *International Journal of Speech Language and the Law* in 2003). This journal has always been shared with the International Association of Forensic Phonetics (established 1991, later renamed the International Association of Forensic Phonetics and Acoustics).

Eades also convened the 1995 meeting of IAFL at the University of New England Armidale, further catalysing interest in forensic applications among Australian linguists – some of whose work is described in this Element.

At Monash University, Heydon began working on research addressing the linguistic dimensions of police interviews with children, a field previously dominated by psychologists (Heydon, 1998, 2005: 148–64). Heydon's work contributed to the development of forensic linguistics in Australia as a complement to psychological research into child cognition and legal interviewing.

Meanwhile, also during the mid-1990s, Australian forensic phonetics was being established on a scientific footing through the work of Phil Rose, Andy Butcher, Helen Fraser, John Ingram and others in the Australian Speech Science and Technology Association (ASSTA), as recounted in Section 3.2.

1.3.4 The Twenty-First Century

By the late 1990s, forensic linguistics and forensic phonetics were well established in Australia, with expanding research across various branches (documented in later sections) and increasing interaction with international colleagues.

A number of students were undertaking postgraduate research, and undergraduate courses in language and law were started at the University of New England and the Australian National University, followed by others, including Macquarie University. While these courses are generally taught within linguistics departments, at Monash University Law School a course entitled 'Language, Communication and the Legal Process' has been developed by forensic linguists Peter Gray and John Gibbons and taught several times in the last decade (Section 6.2). Starting in the 1990s, courses in legal interpreting have been taught at Western Sydney University (formerly the University of Western Sydney), the University of New South Wales and RMIT University, among others.

There is now a new generation of forensic linguists, whose early career research is already being published, including Alex Bowen (Sections 3.6.3, 5.1 and 5.2), Alexandra Grey (Section 3.7), Ben Grimes (Sections 3.5.2 and 6.2), Elyse Methven (Section 3.7), Laura Smith-Khan (Section 4.2.4), Yuko Kinoshita (Sections 3.1.2 and 3.2.5), Shunichi Ishihara (Sections 3.2.4 and 3.4) and Miranda Lai (Sections 3.6.2 and 4.1.1). The first five of these came to forensic linguistics with legal training and experience (see Section 2.1).

The most recent development is the establishment in 2020 of the Research Hub for Language in Forensic Evidence at the University of Melbourne (Section 3.1.4).

1.4 Characteristics of Forensic Linguistics in Australia

1.4.1 Beyond Merely 'Applying' Linguistic Knowledge

Not all the questions for which forensic linguists use their expertise can be fully answered simply by 'applying' well-established research findings from linguistic theory. Throughout this Element, readers will see that a key feature of both branches of forensic linguistics in Australia (as in some other countries) is the way that linguists' work both draws on existing research and leads to new research. Indeed, Australian linguists, like some others, have used forensic linguistics to enrich linguistic science more generally.

One way this can happen is via case studies which provide opportunities for analysis of primary data that might not otherwise be available to the linguistic researchers. Eades' work on the Condren case, for example, resulted in clear evidence of the importance of including pragmatic features in the definition of Aboriginal English (Eades, 1993).

In addition, some questions on which linguists are asked to provide expert evidence in court require the discipline not just to apply existing knowledge but to generate new knowledge. For example, while linguists have long-standing knowledge about the pronunciation differences that characterise regional accents of various languages, there is far less work looking at the extent to which those characteristics enable linguists and others to accurately identify speakers from particular regions (Section 3.3). The latter is an issue that came to prominence with the implementation of language 'tests' for asylum seekers from the 1990s (Fraser, 2009).

Readers will note that the concept of context is relevant to almost every section of this Element. This reflects the central role of context in many branches of linguistics. While we can follow leading sociolinguist Jan Blommaert (2005: 251) in defining context broadly as 'the totality of conditions' in which language is being 'produced, circulated and interpreted', different branches pick out different aspects of context as a focus. An important consideration in analysis of language used as forensic evidence is that context also 'primes' the analyst's interpretation of the evidence. While reliable context primes analysts in helpful ways that are necessary to reliable interpretation, it is essential to guard against exposure to potentially misleading context (Section 3).

1.4.2 Direct Engagement between Linguists and Judicial Officers

A prominent feature of forensic linguistics in Australia is extensive direct engagement between linguists and the judiciary (Section 6). This started with workshops and publications seeking to inform lawyers and judges regarding findings of linguistics that demonstrate the problematic nature of some of the attitudes and beliefs embodied in the law as 'linguistic ideologies' (discussed in more detail below).

Diana Eades and Sandra Hale have been especially prominent in this area. As discussed in Section 6, engagement like this has generally been well received in Australia. For example, both Eades and Hale have worked directly with the law to recommend legal practices and procedures for improving opportunities for equality before the law, for example, Eades (1992), and Hale in the *Recommended National Standards for Working with Interpreters in Courts and Tribunals* (JCCD, 2022, hereafter *National Standards*). (See Sections 2.3.3 and 4.2.1.)

Later their work became an inspiration for the 'Call to Action', in which all four national linguistics bodies called on the judiciary to review and reform the handling of indistinct covert recordings used as evidence in criminal trials, as recounted in Section 3. This eventually led to creation of the Research Hub for Language in Forensic Evidence at the University of Melbourne (Section 3.1.4). In October 2022, a workshop of judges, lawyers and linguists convened by the Hub, in collaboration with Deakin Law School, resolved to pursue appropriate reform of legal procedures regarding covert recordings.

1.4.3 Research on Misconceptions and Ideologies

Concern about the effect of misconceptions and problematic language ideologies has grown beyond documenting and addressing individual problems. In Australia, as elsewhere, some linguists (e.g. Eades, 2012; Fraser, 2018; Smith-Khan, 2022) have chosen not just to address them but to make them a topic of study in their own right.

These linguists have undertaken research directly focusing on the misconceptions and ideologies themselves, documenting exactly how they can contribute to injustice and unfairness before the law and recommending appropriate changes that can be made. As analysing and exploring the nature of linguistic misconceptions and problematic language ideologies has become such a prominent feature of Australian forensic linguistics, we devote a separate section to it, next.

2 Misconceptions and Problematic Ideologies

As we have seen, forensic linguistics poses many new and challenging questions for researchers, practitioners and end users. These challenges are substantially increased by misconceptions and problematic ideologies within the law, as mentioned in Section 1.4.3 and discussed in more detail in the remainder of this section.

Before getting to those topics, however, it is worth noting another issue: misconceptions in linguistics about the law. Though this has not yet been so well researched, it is an important theme in several parts of this Element. Together, these mutual misconceptions create significant difficulties for effective communication between linguistics and the law, which Australian forensic linguists, with international colleagues, have been at pains to overcome.

2.1 Misconceptions in Linguistics about the Law

Conley, O'Barr and Riner (2019: 135–6) raise the issue of ignorance and misconceptions held by many linguists about how the law works, which they term 'linguists' ideologies of law'. It is somewhat ironic for a discipline so focused on context, that linguistic work on language in the law often ignores important aspects of the specific legal context being analysed.

For linguists to make a contribution to understanding of the impact of language use in court, it is important to know how the law works, yet this knowledge is sometimes incomplete. For example, at conferences it is common for linguists to express outrage about manipulative questions posed to witnesses during cross-examination. However, this must be understood in the context that defence lawyers are professionally required 'to represent their client's case vigorously and to put all relevant propositions to a witness' (Bowden, Henning & Plater, 2014: 554). Similarly, when a defence lawyer is representing a client who has pleaded not guilty, that lawyer may be legally obliged to challenge the truthfulness of the complainant(s).

Arguably, then, when seen in their structural context, defence strategies that challenge or deny a witness's truthfulness go beyond linguistic trickery. These strategies are allowed, even required, as part of the central work of testing a witness's truthfulness or accuracy. (However, note that Eades (2012) discusses how this cross-examination strategy is facilitated by a problematic language ideology, namely that repeated questioning enables the truth to emerge, Section 4.2.3.)

Another issue, also raised by Conley et al. (2019: 135–6), is an occasional tendency of some linguists to assume that an 'underdog' from a disadvantaged group is necessarily telling the truth (Fraser (2011) discusses several examples). Of course, systemic disadvantage is a very serious issue that many in forensic linguistics strive to overcome. However, it is important to distinguish disadvantage experienced at a group level by members of particular communities, from evaluation of evidence in each individual case.

One final point to mention mostly affects branches of forensic linguistics that provide scientific evidence about language used as evidence in court. Linguists are sometimes dismayed that the law does not simply accept their evidence-based opinion, but leaves decisions for the jury, under the guidance of barristers and judges, who may also take evidence from less qualified witnesses. This is because the law does not itself operate on scientific principles – indeed, the questions a trial addresses are often not capable of being resolved by a purely scientific approach. It does mean, however, that there can sometimes be problems in communicating scientific findings to the court – making it important for experts to consider how best to ensure not only that they themselves reach a reliable opinion about the evidence they are analysing, but also that the court is able to understand their opinion and use it appropriately. Some examples are discussed in Section 3.

Fortunately, Australia is one of the countries where the presence of forensic linguists with legal qualifications and experience is much valued, as is the increasing openness of many legal professionals to engaging in meaningful dialogue with linguists about language in the law.

2.2 Misconceptions in the Law about Language and Speech

2.2.1 Pre-Existing 'Common Knowledge'

With only rare exceptions, all human beings can use spoken (or sometimes signed) language with great skill. It is often assumed that this skill implies underlying knowledge. However, there can be a disjunction between skill in using spoken and written language, and knowledge about how language works. This is similar to the famous observation that one can ride a bicycle without understanding the physics of how the bicycle works. However, the situation with language is worse than just lack of knowledge.

In western society, nearly everyone learns a basic stock of 'facts' about language through school education, especially literacy acquisition. For example:

- speech is a sequence of words, each composed of a sequence of 'sounds' which can be represented with written symbols
- words have fixed meanings, which can be looked up in a dictionary
- different languages represent the same meanings but with different words
- good grammar follows rules of logic
- effective communication results from sending a clear message
- people from different places speak in definably different ways

The problem is that some of the information about language imparted by school education has limited validity. For example, while the dot points above are accepted by many as basic facts about speech, all are recognised in linguistics as being at best partially true. Some are considered to have the status of myths, researched in specialised branches sometimes called 'folk linguistics'. Misconceptions like these can be very hard to overcome. As teachers of linguistics at university level know, it can take years of study to recognise their fallacy.

The existence of such misconceptions does not affect the everyday skills of using language, but it can cause problems when the inaccurate knowledge is used for practical applications.

2.2.2 Lawyers' Knowledge about Language vs Linguists' Expertise

Higher education, especially in the professions, brings increased skill with spoken and written language, and increased knowledge about language, e.g. advanced spelling, grammar, etymology, knowledge of additional languages. However, unless it involves advanced study in linguistics, higher education typically deepens and elaborates the basic misconceptions of common know-ledge rather than overturning them in line with the research findings of linguistic science.

Thus lawyers often have high level skills in the use of spoken and written language, and a strong sense of confidence in their knowledge about language. This is valuable in their profession, which depends heavily on language. However, it is different from the scientific orientation of linguists, who treat language as an object of study.

Indeed, in the early days of forensic linguistics many lawyers did not really know what linguistics was – thinking of a linguist as a polyglot, or as a grammarian enforcing proper usage (not realising linguistics takes a descriptive, rather than a prescriptive, approach). Now, however, there is far more recognition in the law of linguistics as a science – though this may involve a sense that it merely adds technical detail to common knowledge, without full recognition of the extent to which scientific findings can undermine apparent facts of common knowledge. The effect is that lawyers can sometimes feel free to override the opinion of an expert linguist. Some examples are discussed in Section 3.

2.3 Problematic Language Ideologies

2.3.1 Definitions

Widely held views about language are referred to in sociolinguistics and linguistic anthropology as language ideologies, which can be defined as 'meta-level ideas about language' (Ford & Mertz, 2016: 10) or taken-for-granted assumptions about how language works that are socially, culturally and historically conditioned (following Blommaert, 2005: 253).

Language ideologies are typically accepted as basic common sense, but, like the common knowledge discussed above, they can be at odds with the findings of linguistic research. They are often accompanied by, or give rise to, practices (or ways of doing things) which are considered normal within particular social groups, in the sense that they are accepted without need for explanation or justification.

As mentioned above, Australian forensic linguists have studied a number of language ideologies in the legal process, many of which are not limited to the law. The focus of these studies is on how specific practices enabled by these assumptions about language can contribute to, or lead to, unequal or unfair treatment within the law of some individuals or some members of certain groups. This can create tension between the law and other institutions, and within the law, as social values evolve to embrace improved standards of fairness and inclusiveness.

The main language ideologies discussed in this Element are introduced below, as a frame for the coming discussion (see also Sections 4.2.3 and 4.2.4). This is just one way to enumerate and characterise language ideologies; others might classify them differently. Indeed, some scholars might discuss some of the misconceptions we have noted above within a language ideology framework. Here, however, we prefer to maintain the distinction between misconceptions and ideologies.

2.3.2 The Language Expertise Ideology

The language expertise ideology is related to, but different from, the issue of lawyers' incomplete knowledge about linguistics discussed in Section 2.2.2. The language expertise ideology involves the assumption that skill in using a language necessarily implies the language user has explicit and reliable knowledge about the structure and usage of the language.

In relation to English language, this ideology underlies the legal expectation that juries can make their own evaluation of language evidence, without need for expert evidence. Examples are given in Section 3.1 and 3.2 of legal procedures that encourage juries to reach their own opinions, even if their view contradicts the opinion of an expert.

In relation to languages other than English, this ideology means the status of expert can be given simply on the basis of ability to speak the language. For example, witnesses can be asked to give an expert opinion purely on the basis of being a native speaker of the language (Sections 3.2.5 and 3.3).

2.3.3 Monolingual Language Ideology

A language ideology in many English-speaking countries, including Australia, is the assumption that monolingualism is, and should be, the norm in society. This is despite evidence that multilingualism is more prevalent in societies around the world than monolingualism.

This monolingual language ideology creates a range of problems, some stemming from poor understanding of what is involved in learning a language, or in living in a country where one has lower proficiency in the standard language. One effect noted by Australian forensic linguists is lack of sensitivity in the law to the difference between ability to produce a few words of English in answer to simple questions, and ability to participate fully in English-based legal proceedings.

As Section 3.6 will show, a number of Australian linguists have worked to counter this assumption. In particular, a correction to it underlies the results of Sandra Hale's linguistic work on the JCCD (2022) *National Standards* (Section 1.4.2). Thus, part of Standard 16 for Judicial Officers advises them not to rely on 'the ... ability [of a person who speaks English as a second language] to provide biographical data as the basis for deciding whether to work with an interpreter'. This is because

> it does not necessarily follow from the fact that a person can adequately answer simple questions about their life [in English] that they have sufficient English proficiency to understand court proceedings, discuss legal concepts, or listen to and give evidence in court. (JCCD, 2022: 62)

Over recent years the legal system has made considerable progress in recognising that many Australians, both immigrant and Indigenous, need interpreters in order to understand and participate in the law. The *National Standards* document is arguably the clearest evidence of this progress. However, this is only a partial antidote to the monolingual language ideology. The assumption that monolingualism *should be* the norm is still widespread, and it is seen in a number of ways in the legal system, to be discussed in Section 3.6.

2.3.4 Written Language Ideology

Many ideologies that affect forensic linguistics can be seen as part of a larger societal ideology, with effects far beyond the law, that privileges written language as the basic form of linguistic expression (Olson, 1994).

Although the law is often conducted in spoken language, it places a strong emphasis on written language, which is considered more stable and more 'real' than ephemeral spoken language. This is seen explicitly in the importance placed on written contracts and other legal instruments. However, it is implicitly involved in the priority given to transcripts of spoken language, including court proceedings, police interviews and many other events in the legal process (Deamer et al., 2022).

The law has a rather unsophisticated view of the relationship between the transcript and the spoken language it represents, which are often seen as transposable analogues of one another (Haworth, 2018; Fraser, 2022a). In legal contexts this written language ideology can thus give rise to what Walsh (1995) calls 'the tyranny of the transcript'.

The priority given to written language also has the effect, again seen in many areas within and beyond the law, that spoken communication is seen as message transfer, almost like sending a written note. This idea has been well studied as the 'conduit metaphor' (see Lakoff & Johnson, 1980). The conduit metaphor creates the impression that the message is fixed, and simply travels from sender to receiver. This has been shown to be unrealistic, even for written language but especially for spoken language. Communication really involves the receiver making meaning of the message, which may align with the sender's meaning to a greater or lesser extent (Liddicoat & Haugh, 2009).

The conduit metaphor has been extended into the area of interpreting and translation, where it is useful in understanding a range of misconceptions about what is involved in rendering one language into another. For example, the conduit metaphor suggests, wrongly, that interpreters and translators simply exchange words and sentences from one language into another (see Hale, 2004; Nakane, 2014; Fraser 2022a). This has a major negative effect in the legal process, especially when combined with the monolingual ideology (Sections 3.6 and 5.2).

2.3.5 Referential Language Ideology

The referential ideology of language sees language as a fixed and transparent means of reference, as being 'stable, denotational and context-free' (Ehrlich, 2012: 58; Eades 2012; 2016a; Ehrlich & Eades 2016). In this view of language, one of the simplest words in the English language, 'yes', when given in answer to a question seeking confirmation of a proposition, must always signal agreement to the proposition – because the meaning of 'yes' is taken to be stable, signalling agreement, and no contextual factors need to be considered in understanding its use in a particular answer. Despite the widespread operation of this referential language ideology in the law, we do not claim it is universal (for some exceptions see examples from judgments in Sections 3.5.1 and 3.6.1).

The view of language as having fixed meaning is aligned with the assumption (related to the conduit metaphor) that the primary function of language is to transmit information. This ignores the wide range of functions that language is used for, and the ways in which the meaning of an utterance can change depending on context (consider, for example, requesting, commanding, being sarcastic or joking).

To conclude Section 2, linguistic research in legal settings and linguistic expert evidence in specific cases highlight the central role of context in the workings of language.

For this reason, we have structured our report of the work of Australian forensic linguists in the next three sections in terms of linguistic, interactional and sociocultural contexts of the language data being analysed. We recognise that distinction of the three contexts is not always clear-cut and there is unavoidable overlap between the sections. This categorisation should be seen as one way of organising the material in a necessarily linear publication, but not the only way.

3 Linguistic Contexts

This section examines forensic linguistics that involves analysis of the linguistic context of the language data, using expertise in phonetics, syntax, semantics and other analytical branches of linguistic science. The subsections cover most of the branches of forensic linguistics in which Australian linguists have engaged most fully, including forensic transcription, forensic speaker recognition, forensic authorship analysis, the study of legal language and issues that arise from diversity in linguistic repertoire, with a focus on the participation in legal processes of people who use standard English as a second language or second dialect.

3.1 Forensic Transcription

3.1.1 Legal History of Forensic Transcription

During the late 1970s, it became legal (under strict regulation) for police investigating serious crimes to use hidden listening devices to obtain covert (secret) recordings of suspects' conversations. While these recordings were crucial during investigations, it soon became clear that they also had value as evidence in court. The first case in Australasia, and possibly in the world, where the prosecution sought to have this kind of surveillance audio admitted as evidence was a 1981 drugs trial in New Zealand (see Fraser, 2021 for details on the case and the following history).

The problem was that the audio was of such poor quality that the jury could not understand what was said, even after hearing it played through twice. The prosecution offered a transcript prepared by police. Initially, the judge refused to admit this as it conflicted with multiple legal principles. As one example, the law considers a transcript to be an opinion as to the content of the audio – and police are generally not allowed to provide opinions in court, only factual evidence.

However, when the judge tried listening to the audio with the transcript, he found it so helpful that he agreed it should be provided to assist the jury in understanding the content of the recording, which, if they accepted the transcript, was relevant and probative evidence. This required adjusting the legal principles he had cited earlier. For example, since opinions can be given by experts, police transcribers were deemed to have a kind of ad hoc expertise, on the grounds that their ability to understand indistinct audio came from listening many times. These adjustments were upheld on appeal (*R v Menzies* 1982), and the case became a precedent allowing police transcripts to be provided to assist juries' perception of indistinct covert recordings in many subsequent trials.

It is important for linguists to understand that police transcripts are not given directly to the jury. The law is well aware that a detective's hearing might not always be accurate, and has developed a series of safeguards to ensure juries are not misled by an inaccurate transcript. Defence lawyers are expected to review transcripts and negotiate with the prosecution to create an agreed version for the jury. If agreement cannot be reached, the judge listens personally to ensure nothing potentially misleading goes to the jury. Finally, the judge instructs the jury that the evidence is the audio not the transcript, so they should listen carefully and reach their own conclusion about the audio content, using the transcript only as assistance (the 'aide memoire' instruction).

In 1987, these procedures were endorsed by the High Court of Australia (*Butera v DPP (VIC)* 1987), and eventually accommodated by the Uniform Evidence Acts that most Australian jurisdictions passed from 1995. Over the following decades, the use of covert surveillance spread rapidly, and the procedures became fully embedded across many branches of law and law enforcement. From a legal perspective, they are now completely standard, used routinely not just for covert recordings but for other types of forensic audio. However, from the perspective of linguistic science, they are problematic.

The procedures rest on the assumption that understanding spoken language is a matter of common knowledge (Section 2.2.1). This is why determining the content of audio evidence is considered a matter for juries, while development of safeguards to ensure juries are not exposed to potentially misleading transcripts is undertaken by judges. The problem is that, while understanding spoken language is certainly a common skill, knowledge about how that skill works, especially about the factors that affect perception of indistinct recorded speech, requires highly specialised scientific expertise (Fraser & Loakes, 2020). Without that expertise, the law cannot effectively prevent listeners, including juries, from gaining confident, but inaccurate, perception of the audio, with potential impact on the verdict. In particular, the safeguards developed through legal precedent are not nearly as trustworthy as they seem to lawyers.

3.1.2 Involvement of Linguistic Science

Since the 1990s, the advice of experts has increasingly been sought when prosecution and defence cannot reach agreement on some part of a transcript (see French & Fraser, 2018), and evidence on disputed utterances has been given by Felicity Cox, Helen Fraser, Phil Rose and Andy Butcher, among others.

Through this kind of casework, Fraser developed concerns about the risk to justice posed by use of police transcripts, and especially about the assumption that the aide memoire instruction could ensure juries were not misled if the transcript happened to be inaccurate (see Fraser, 2020b for more on this history). She led a 2011 experiment using audio from a real murder trial, demonstrating how easily an inaccurate transcript can mislead listeners into 'hearing' incriminating words which had not actually been spoken (see Fraser & Kinoshita, 2021). This experiment attracted interest and concern from linguists – but lawyers were not disturbed. They trusted the safeguards, especially the concept that if the transcript was wrong, the defence would dispute it, and the judge would check it personally against the audio. The problem here is that even responsible listeners like judges can be misled by an inaccurate transcript.

This was forcefully demonstrated by another murder trial that came to Fraser in 2011. She showed that a police transcript that had passed all the legal safeguards, and been provided to 'assist' the jury, was actually misleading. In collaboration with psychologist Bruce Stevenson, she then used the audio in an experiment, showing that the lawyers and judges who checked the inaccurate police transcript must themselves have been unwittingly misled by it. This cast doubt, not only on the justice of the conviction, but also on the value of the safeguards (Fraser, 2018). Fraser (2013) argued that the situation effectively continued the possibility of verballing, supposed to have been eradicated by the introduction of recorded police interviews (Section 1.2.2).

Though it was too late for an appeal in this case, Fraser's results were used for an application to review the conviction. The application was rejected on the grounds that legal procedures had been followed properly, so the jury were able to make up their own minds about the evidence (Fraser, 2018). This marked a turning point in Fraser's understanding of the causes of inaccurate transcription of indistinct covert recordings. It was now clear that the key problem with the legal handling of indistinct covert recordings was not the fact that transcripts are produced by police (though that is far from ideal). It was the fact that all transcripts, by police or experts, are evaluated by lawyers and judges, on the assumption that detecting and correcting errors requires only common knowledge. Fraser sought opportunities to explain scientific facts about perception of indistinct audio to the law. Through this work, additional problems with covert recordings were also uncovered. Particular risks were noted with lax procedures for admitting translations of indistinct audio featuring languages other than English. Other concerns included inaccuracy in attributing utterances represented in a transcript to particular speakers, and admission of 'enhanced' versions of indistinct audio.

3.1.3 The 'Call to Action'

Fraser sought advice from the Australian Linguistics Society (ALS), who recommended a 'Call to Action'. This was a 2017 letter, endorsed by four national organisations (ALS, ALAA, ASSTA and AusIT), asking the Australian judiciary to review and reform legal procedures for admitting indistinct covert recordings as evidence in criminal trials. The letter was delivered to Professor Greg Reinhardt, then Executive Director of the Australasian Institute of Judicial Administration (AIJA), who forwarded it to the Council of Chief Justices (CCJ). The CCJ assigned the 'Call' to Chief Justice Chris Kourakis, Chair of the Judicial Council on Cultural Diversity (JCCD), the body which had provided strong leadership on linguistic matters in the past (Section 2.3.3). In late 2019 a working group of four JCCD judges (Section 6.2) held an extended consultation with linguists Helen Fraser, Diana Eades, Georgina Heydon, Alex Bowen, Lesley Stirling (then President of ALS) and Peter Gray (see Section 6.2). Representatives from police and prosecution departments around the country were also invited.

At the end of the consultation, the JCCD judges acknowledged that the problems outlined by the linguists needed investigation, and in early 2020, the University of Melbourne's Faculty of Arts established the Research Hub for

Language in Forensic Evidence in their School of Languages and Linguistics, with Helen Fraser as Director and Debbie Loakes as Research Fellow (Fraser, 2020a).

3.1.4 The Research Hub for Language in Forensic Evidence

In relation to forensic transcription, the Hub has two main aims. The first is to assist in reforming legal procedures to ensure that all indistinct audio admitted as evidence is accompanied by a demonstrably reliable transcript right from the start of the trial process. The second is to develop accountable evidence-based methods for creating reliable transcripts of indistinct forensic audio – for both English and other languages. This requires more than just applying existing scientific knowledge (Section 1.4.1). Although transcripts are used extensively in many branches of linguistic science, linguists rarely transcribe indistinct audio in situations where they do not know the content, and where the context is potentially misleading – which is the situation faced in forensic transcription (Fraser, 2022b). To ensure reliability, it is necessary to pursue cross-disciplinary research questions focused on demonstrating the capabilities of transcribers, not just on analysing the acoustic-phonetic properties of speech (see Fraser 2020a, 2022b for detailed discussion).

The problem is that no matter how good such evidence-based methods become, they cannot, on their own, ensure that juries are only assisted by reliable transcripts – since current legal procedures prioritise police transcripts even where they have been shown to be inaccurate by an expert on their own side (Fraser, 2021). Law reform, though challenging, is essential.

In developing these ideas, it has become clear that, in addition to the situations described above, transcripts are used in concerning ways across other legal contexts (cf. Haworth, 2018; Deamer et al., 2022). This provides more evidence of the negative influence of misconceptions arising from the written language ideology (Sections 2.2, 2.3.4).

3.2 Forensic Speaker Recognition

3.2.1 From Ear Witnesses to Forensic Audio

One way spoken language can be used as forensic evidence is to identify a speaker involved in a crime when visual recognition is not possible (e.g. if perpetrators wear masks). Traditionally, such evidence could only be given by a listener who had heard the voice live – an 'ear witness'. Ear witnesses have long been allowed to testify in court, and their evidence is highly compelling. However, it is now known to be prone to error, with memory for voices even more unreliable than the poor visual memory of eyewitnesses, responsible for many miscarriages of justice (for more details see Fraser, 2019). Nevertheless, ear witness evidence is still allowed in courts around the world, including Australia (McGorrery & McMahon, 2016).

The rise of recording technology meant that in some cases voices were preserved (e.g. on a telephone answering machine). This reduced reliance on memory and extended the role of ear witness to listeners who were not present at the time. It also meant that juries, rather than relying on witness testimony, could now listen 'with their own ears', comparing the voice on the tape to that of the alleged speaker.

Further, they could be assisted in their judgment by testimony from witnesses familiar with the alleged speaker's voice. Such witnesses included police reviewing surveillance audio – and the status of 'ad hoc expert' (Section 3.1.1) was soon extended to cover speaker identification, with safeguards similar to those used for police transcripts (Chan, 2020).

As with forensic transcription, the law considers speaker recognition to be a topic of common knowledge. Again, however, while listeners confidently identify speakers in everyday situations, scientific studies show that this skill relies on context far more than listeners realise. When voices are heard out of context, as in a recording, recognition performance is surprisingly poor; more importantly, when voices are heard in a misleading context, they can be identified confidently but wrongly (see Kreiman & Sidtis, 2011: Chapter 7).

3.2.2 Early Use of Expert Witnesses

A further benefit of forensic audio was that it allowed investigators to commission expert assistance in profiling unknown speakers whose voices had been captured in audio. This approach had an early and dramatic start in Australia, with the infamous 1971 Qantas bomb hoax (the Wikipedia article '1971 Qantas bomb hoax' provides a good introduction). A caller identifying himself as 'Mr Brown' left a message that a plane, in flight from Sydney to Hong Kong, had been planted with a bomb set to explode when the plane passed below a certain altitude. Authorities were unable to locate the bomb, or the bomber, so were forced to hand over a large cash ransom. After the ransom was paid, they were told there was no bomb: it had all been a hoax.

Police mounted a national manhunt. With no hard evidence, they explored every line of enquiry. Since some of the phone calls had been recorded, they asked a member of Sydney University's English Department, Alex Jones, to assist in identifying the speaker's accent. Jones reached the conclusion that the hoaxer was English, possibly from Cornwall.

Authorities enlisted the aid of Scotland Yard, but still the hoaxer could not be found – until his accomplice visited the local petrol station driving a series of expensive cars. Attendants reported him to police, and he quickly confessed his involvement, naming the mastermind as Peter Macari, an Englishman originally from Devon, now living in Australia. Macari initially denied involvement, but eventually police gathered compelling evidence against him, and he too confessed. This meant there was no trial, so Jones' evidence was never tested in court – but the case brought his field to the attention of police, who called on him for other bomb threat cases, prevalent at the time, as well as for other types of analysis (see Jones, 1994).

Sometimes Jones appeared for the defence. In one case, involving recordings of menacing telephone calls, he formed the view, on the basis of auditory analysis, that the suspect was not the speaker in the audio. To back up his opinion, he obtained a recording of the suspect reading the same words, and compared the voices with the aid of spectrograms (visual representations of speech, widely used in phonetics research). In the trial, the judge disallowed Jones' evidence, as the courts did not recognise phonetics as a field of expertise. However, that decision was overturned when an appeal (*R v Gilmore* 1977) cited cases from the US where spectrograms had been admitted as 'voiceprint' evidence.

This raised protest from a police sound engineer, who published an article (Hall & Collins, 1980) pointing out that the voiceprint evidence used in US courts was a known pseudoscience. This is true (see IAFPA's 'Voiceprint Resolution': iafpa.net/about/resolutions/). However, though Jones' use of spectrograms would not be considered valid forensic phonetics today, it was not voiceprint evidence in the US sense. The terms 'voiceprint' and 'spectrogram' refer to the same thing, but the way they are used is very different (Hammarström, 1987). Voiceprint methods were developed by engineers on the mistaken assumption that voices have unique characteristics, like fingerprints. Spectrographic analysis was, and remains, an important tool for responsible phonetic analysis of all kinds.

It is interesting to note that, despite their opposition to Jones' evidence for the defence in *Gilmore*, police commissioned him to provide spectrographic evidence for subsequent trials, including that of the infamous 'Woolworths bombers' (*R v McHardie & Danielson* 1983), which is still cited as a precedent, though the methods are not approved by the current science of forensic phonetics.

3.2.3 A Growing Field

Though Alex Jones was the first linguist to provide speaker identification evidence in Australia, others gradually followed (see Eades, 1994). Göran Hammarström, of Monash University, was an early practitioner (Hammarström, 1987). In 1988, following Hammarström's retirement, Heather Bowe established the Monash Speaker Identification Unit, through which Kate Storey and others undertook case work (Bowe & Storey, 1995).

Around 1993, another infamous trial drew more phoneticians into forensics. Threatening phone calls, in fake Italian or Chinese accents, were received by NSW government and media offices, and office workers claimed to recognise the voice of local politician Barry Morris. Experts were instructed by both sides. While some provided evidence confirming the office workers' views, Helen Fraser took a more cautious approach, for two reasons.

First, she noted that the office workers, as ear witnesses, were not reliable. To demonstrate this, she ran a small experiment in which listeners attempted to recognise voices of colleagues and family members without contextual information. To participants' surprise, no one scored 100 per cent. Even for undisguised voices, most scored around 80–90 per cent, and confidence correlated poorly with accuracy. For disguised voices, scores were far lower, often at chance (in line with studies later reported in Kreiman & Sidtis, 2011). This made it likely that the office workers were not recognising Morris by voice alone, but were being influenced by contextual assumptions (see also Jones, 1994).

Second, Fraser argued that phonetic science had not yet developed methods capable of reliably identifying speakers from their voices, especially with short samples of disguised speech. In the mid-1990s, the science of speaker recognition was in its infancy (see Nolan, 1983; Baldwin & French, 1990). Fraser sought to publicise the limitations of speaker recognition in police and legal newsletters – hoping that the information would enable the law to take a more realistic approach – and also presented her experience with the Barry Morris recordings in a special session at the 1995 IAFL conference at University of New England.

3.2.4 A Developing Science

Other phoneticians were experiencing similar concerns (cf. Rose & Duncan, 1995). By the mid-1990s, demand for forensic speaker identification expertise, previously sporadic, was burgeoning. This was due to an unintended side effect of the requirement that all police interviews with suspects should be recorded (Section 1.2.2). Where previously it had been rare to have an appropriate known sample of a voice to compare with a speaker heard in forensic audio, recorded interviews meant a known sample was now available for almost every case (cf. French, 2017).

However, demand was not always being filled by properly qualified experts in phonetic science. In fact, despite the cases mentioned above, the courts often disallowed evidence from phoneticians in the belief that their expertise added nothing to the common knowledge already possessed by the jury. Some judges even preferred evidence from engineers, seeing this as more 'scientific' than phonetics.

Concerned by the poor quality of speaker recognition evidence, a group of ASSTA members established a Forensic Speech Science Standards Committee (FSSSC) aiming to develop standards to ensure that forensic speaker recognition was carried out by properly qualified experts. Founding members included John Ingram (chair), Phil Rose, Andy Butcher, Michael Wagner, Helen Fraser and Laura Tollfree.

To help upskill phoneticians in this new application of their science, Rose convened a 1996 seminar led by Francis Nolan of the University of Cambridge, one of the first phoneticians to study the phonetic bases of speaker recognition (Nolan, 1983). ASSTA conferences started to have sessions on forensic phonetics, and several researchers and students started working on forensic speaker recognition (e.g. Ingram, Prandolini & Ong, 1996). Also around this time, Laura Tollfree joined Monash University linguistics department, undertaking substantial, well-regarded research. However, while she inspired several students to take up forensic phonetics (see Loakes, 2008; Loakes & McDougall, 2010), Tollfree herself left academia around 2000. Australian phonetician Duncan Markham, working overseas mainly on second language pronunciation, also contributed casework and research (Markham, 1999).

3.2.5 The Paradigm Shift

A major development was sparked by Hugh Selby, then at the Australian National University Law School, who commissioned Phil Rose to write a chapter on forensic speaker identification (see Freckelton & Selby, 2019). Selby gave Rose the first (1995) edition of *Interpreting Evidence* (Robertson, Vignaux & Berger, 2016), which explained the need for the forensic sciences to use Bayesian statistics, especially Likelihood Ratio (LR). This important book had a powerful influence on Rose, who became a strong advocate for use of LR in speaker comparison (Rose 2002), undertaking extensive research in this area and giving LR evidence in a number of high-profile cases (see https://philjohn rose.net).

Rose trained several graduate students in the use of LR, including Tony Alderman (2005), Jennifer Elliot, Yuko Kinoshita and Shunichi Ishihara. He also brought Geoffrey Morrison from Canada as a research associate on a large ARC Discovery Project (2007–2010). Morrison then led an ARC Linkage project (2010–2013) through UNSW's School of Electrical

Engineering and Telecommunications, and later took a senior position at Aston Institute for Forensic Linguistics in England. From there he has been influential in gaining support from forensic scientists for use of LR in speaker comparison (e.g. Morrison et al., 2021). Within forensic phonetics itself, however, though Rose's Bayesian insights have been well accepted, it is fair to say that his highly technical and mathematical approach to using LR has been received with less enthusiasm (see responses to Rose & Morrison, 2009; Hudson, McDougall & Hughes, 2021). This may be because, valuable as the concept of LR is, the fact that an expert report contains explicit calculation of an LR is not the only or even the main criterion distinguishing reliable from unreliable speaker comparison evidence. So even if all conclusions were given as a likelihood ratio, the courts could still be misled – for example if the LR is calculated on the basis of unjustified measurements or assumptions (Fraser, 2012).

Another major problem, explored with some sensitivity by Rose (2013), is the difficulty of explaining the mathematics of his LR approach, and the abstract acoustic analyses it favours, to the courts. As a result, these concepts have, to date, had little impact in reducing reliance on ad hoc experts for voice evidence in Australian courts – indeed this has expanded, with interpreters and translators now allowed to offer opinions regarding the identity of speakers of languages other than English (Chan, 2020).

Further, outside the excellent, but rather technical, work of Rose's group (e.g. Kinoshita & Ishihara, 2015), few Australian phoneticians have continued research, teaching or practice in forensic speaker comparison (though Kirsty McDougall has been a prolific researcher at the University of Cambridge, England). This means the pool of genuine experts available locally to give speaker comparison evidence is very small, with some indication that demand is being filled by less qualified personnel.

3.2.6 Looking Forward

Rose's (2002) book is rightly valued for bringing the crucial concepts of Bayesian reasoning to forensic speaker recognition. However, the focus on the mathematics of LR may have left the most important Bayesian insights obscure to some.

Perhaps these key insights can be clarified by considering why a Bayesian approach is so essential to forensic analysis in the first place. The forensic task is significantly different from 'normal' phonetic research, especially in the relationship between what is known and what is being determined. Normally, to investigate speaker characteristics, the analyst starts with known speakers, and studies how their voices vary depending on their known regional, social and other characteristics. In forensic casework, by contrast, the speaker's identity is not known. It must be determined from speech characteristics observable in the audio.

The significance of this difference is highlighted by a useful analogy (cf. Koehler, 2013): if 'normal' phonetic analysis is like determining how likely it is that Jack is eating a meat pie, given that he is known to be at a football match, then forensic casework is like determining how likely it is that Jack is at a football match, given that he is known to be eating a meat pie. These two questions, though they may seem similar on the surface, are fundamentally different. Answering them requires not just different statistics but different methodologies. In particular, the second requires access to information not stated in the question, namely, how often Jack eats pies at venues other than football matches.

Turning the analogy to phonetics, consider, for example, the observation that a certain proportion of Melburnians pronounce 'celery' like 'salary' (see Loakes et al., 2014). Valuable as this information is, it cannot be used directly to determine the likelihood that a recorded speaker who pronounces 'celery' like 'salary' is a particular individual who is known to come from Melbourne. Among other necessary information, the analyst would need to know the proportion of non-Melburnians who pronounce 'celery' like 'salary'; and the proportion of Melburnians who do not (consistently) use this pronunciation. These are complex questions. Answering them in the context of a particular case requires careful consideration of a range of factors spanning multiple branches of linguistic science. Importantly, for many of the factors, quantifiable information is not (yet) available.

Perhaps exploring this more conceptual understanding of Bayesian reasoning can give non-mathematicians better access to its insights, open up a broader set of research questions – and assist in developing accountable, evidence-based methods focusing on developing the capabilities of analysts as well as the discipline's knowledge about speaker differences.

The overarching problem is that, as with forensic transcription (Section 3.1), no matter how good such evidence-based methods might become, as long as current legal procedures remain in place, good scientific methods alone cannot ensure that juries are provided with reliable assistance in determining the identity of speakers in forensic audio. Experts giving speaker comparison opinions are not always aware that a police opinion will likely have been provided to the court before the expert opinion is offered, and that the jury will be explicitly instructed to listen to the audio and reach their own conclusion as to which opinion they prefer – because speaker recognition is still considered by the law to be a matter of common knowledge.

It is essential to ensure that the law treats speaker recognition as a science, and acknowledges that well-established findings show many assumptions of common knowledge are simply incorrect. Equally, speech science must recognise that the law does not operate on scientific principles, and scientific evidence needs to be tailored to the realities of courtroom discourse (Section 2.1).

3.3 LADO

Another branch of forensic linguistics in which Australian scholars have played a role on the international stage is Language Analysis for the Determination of the Origin of asylum seekers, or LADO (now sometimes known as Language Analysis in the Asylum Procedure, or LAAP). This came into use in Europe during the late 1990s, in response to governments' need to decide the refugee status of increasing numbers fleeing persecution and seeking asylum without a passport. Some governments retained qualified linguists to offer expert opinions regarding the regional or social accents of these asylum seekers. However, others used the services of commercial agencies employing native speakers to produce quick-turnaround reports – raising concern among linguists.

When Australia joined the growing number of countries using these European agencies, Diana Eades was contacted by immigration lawyers concerned that unjust decisions were being made on the basis of poor-quality reports. As a result, she led a small group of colleagues in a review of fifty-eight cases heard by the Australian Refugee Review Tribunal (Eades et al., 2003). The review revealed shockingly poor standards of linguistic evidence – in line with similar discoveries made by colleagues in countries around the globe.

Eades and the late Jacques Arends went on to convene an international group of linguists, who developed a set of Guidelines intended to assist governments in choosing appropriate LADO analysts and procedures (Language and National Origin Group, 2004). The Guidelines were authored by nineteen linguists from six countries, including Australians Diana Eades, Helen Fraser, Tim McNamara and Jeff Siegel. The document's key message is that linguistics is a science, with many counterintuitive findings, of which native speakers are typically unaware (Section 2.2). Indeed, the very concept of 'native speaker' is highly problematic (Eades & Arends, 2004; Eades, 2005; Eades, 2009). For these and other reasons, the Guidelines recommended expert opinions on regional and social dialects should be provided by academics with qualifications both in the language in question and in linguistics.

The Guidelines were endorsed by multiple international linguistics organisations, and for several years appeared to be having some good effects (Eades, 2009). However, in 2007 a contrary view was expressed, that LADO was best done by a team including a native speaker of the language in question, without linguistics qualifications, and a linguist, without qualifications in the language in question (see Fraser, 2019 for detailed background). This team approach sparked considerable controversy in the international linguistics community, in which Australian linguists Tim McNamara and Helen Fraser played a prominent role as researchers (see contributions to Zwaan, Muyskin & Verrips, 2010 and Patrick, Schmid & Zwaan, 2019). These discussions raised the important distinction, also referred to in Section 3.2.6, between 'normal' linguistic research, examining the speech patterns of speakers with known regional identity, and forensic casework, seeking to determine speakers' regional identity from their speech patterns (see Fraser, 2009, 2012 for further discussion).

However, by this time Australian governments were no longer using the services of LADO agencies (mainly due to the change to offshore detention). For this reason Australian work directly on LADO has tapered off, though linguists retain a strong interest in assisting asylum-seekers to attain linguistic justice (Section 4.2.4).

3.4 Authorship Attribution

Since Eades (1994) provided an account of the state of forensic linguistics in Australia, surprisingly little has changed with respect to the prevalence of authorship attribution cases in Australian courts. Eades reports one such case (see also Eagleson, 1994), in which Robert Eagleson gave an opinion on the authorship of a letter in 1982 (Court of Petty Sessions, Sydney).

Since that time, although the linguistic analysis of documents has featured in some court cases in Australia, such analysis of authorship is not well documented. The majority of cases in which linguists are consulted never reach the courts, not all legal decisions are publicly reported and not all reported decisions record the presence of an expert (such as Heydon's evidence in *R v Watson* 2009). The low visibility of expert reports on authorship in the court records means that there are fewer opportunities for judges to draw on a precedent when deciding how to treat linguistic expertise on authorship, if it is admitted at all.

Evidence in the academic literature of Australian scholars' engagement with authorship attribution research or casework is similarly limited. Terry Royce (University of Technology, Sydney) has conducted authorship analysis (https://au.linkedin.com/in/terryroyce) but has not published his case reports. Heydon (2019) includes a description of corpus analysis used for authorship analysis in a murder trial in Queensland. However, the forensic linguistic report was ultimately set aside because the defence counsel withdrew their assertion that the defendant had not written the anonymous letter which was the subject of the forensic examination. The method described in Heydon (2019) was one which used a large international corpus of informal written language (the Birmingham Blog Corpus) and compared the frequency of idiosyncratic spellings in the forensic texts with their frequency in the corpus.

Aside from this account of statistical analysis of corpus data for authorship attribution, the main contribution to this field in Australia has come from Shunichi Ishihara at the Australian National University. His research on likelihood ratios in N-gram analysis (2014) and stylometrics (2017) has brought statistical approaches to authorship attribution, or, as Ishihara prefers to describe it, forensic text comparison.

By contrast with Ishihara's reliance on experimental research to support statistically valid methods of analysis and Heydon's corpus analysis approach, the rare examples of legal engagement with forensic linguists for the purposes of authorship attribution has tended towards stylistics (see Heydon 2019: 17), and, as evidenced in *Mason v R* 2015, towards the use of international specialists rather than local linguists. On the other hand, Australian-based Japanese forensic linguist Ikuko Nakane has worked on a 2013 questioned authorship case in Japan. Her stylistic analysis suggested that it was difficult to exclude the possibility that an unknown threatening text message was *not* authored by the writer of a known written text.

Given the scarcity of case reports or court records documenting statistically or scientifically validated methods of authorship analysis, it is important to give due attention in the academic literature to the work of Australian forensic linguists like Ishihara who are publishing findings of their ongoing research into statistically validated authorship attribution methods. Case reports such as Heydon (2019), and Bowen and Eades' (2022) explanation of the difference between forensic linguistics and pseudoscience, are also helpful for the practitioner community to identify the difference between methods that are statistically valid and scientific and those that are not underpinned by a valid scientific foundation.

3.5 Legal Language, Trademarks and Linguistic Evidence about Meaning

International research by linguists and psycholinguists has investigated the problem of legal language, why it is so hard for non-legally trained people to understand, and what can be done to improve the situation. This area has not received much attention from linguistic research in Australia. But it has been a part of the application of linguistics to the law since the work of the late Robert

Eagleson, who is widely recognised as a pioneer of the Plain Language Movement, and particularly its application to the law. Linguists have also written expert reports in cases involving disputes about the interpretation of legal documents and trademarks, and linguistic evidence has been given in a few cases of linguistic evidence about the meaning of (non-legal) language.

3.5.1 Expert Evidence/Casework

While linguists readily identify semantic and pragmatic meaning as linguistic phenomena, suitable for analysis with theories of language structure and use, judges and lawyers might be surprised to find that anyone other than a legally trained and qualified professional could shed light on the meaning of a legal text (Section 2.2.2). This provides the grounds for a contest of ontologies in relation to language and meaning. In law, there has been a reliance on fixed meanings and recourse to 'dictionary definitions' to resolve disputes over meaning, without taking account of context. This is described in Section 2.3.5 as the referential language ideology and underlies a number of misunderstandings about language by legal professionals.

In the current examination of meaning in written legal language, this ideology of referentialism appears to be expressed as a 'turf war', and the example provided below from case law as well as case studies from the authors' own work demonstrate that referentialism is invoked differently by different courts – some judges holding that meaning is fixed regardless of context and therefore a linguist offers no special expertise, while some others find that the linguistic theory being applied in a linguistic report is too abstract and ignores context, thus rendering it irrelevant to the proceedings.

Legal Text Interpretation

When it comes to interpretation of the meaning of legal texts, Solan (1998: 97) has pointed out that a linguist 'doesn't know better than laypeople what ordinary English words and expressions mean'. But the linguist can 'bring to the [trier of fact's] attention a range of possible interpretations that is available to everyone, but which might have gone unnoticed' (ibid.). To this extent, the report of a linguist on the analysis of meaning might be at odds with legal interpretation and the basis of the contest sometimes reflects the referentialism of legal language. This is seen in a long-running and complex bankruptcy case before the Federal Court of Australia, *Australian Prudential Regulation Authority v Siminton* 2007. In this case, the court rejected the expert evidence of the linguist (Heydon) while at the same time allowing counsel for the respondent (who had sought to introduce the linguistic expert report) to rely on the contentions of the linguistic analysis in their argument. It is worth noting that Heydon's analysis was greatly simplified when presented by counsel, as described in paragraph 44 below (emphasis added):

> 43 Counsel for Mr Siminton sought to introduce expert evidence from a linguist as to how an ordinary person would construe the words 'the moneys standing to the credit of the respondent' in Order 1(e). It was these moneys which Mr Siminton was prevented from dealing with. The expert opinion was that a reader of the order would understand it to apply to moneys which were in the relevant accounts on the date on which the order was made – 10 January 2006 and not moneys thereafter added. **I rejected the tender of this evidence because the proper construction of Order 1(e) was a matter of law, not a matter of fact.**

> 44 I allowed counsel to pursue an argument that, as a matter of law, the order was to be construed and understood in the manner contended for by the expert. As developed the submission was that 'the moneys' was a reference to a definite article. When read in conjunction with 'standing' the use of the present tense meant that the relevant moneys were those in the relevant accounts on 10 January 2006 rather than 'future moneys' in 'future accounts'.

This excerpt demonstrates that Australian courts can acknowledge the worthiness of the linguistic perspective on the matter, but find that interpretation of an order is a legal matter, and not relevant for expert linguistic analysis, as noted in the highlighted sentence above. Further details about this case can be found in the decision and in Heydon (2019).

Trademark Infringement Cases

There are few instances of trademark disputes resolved with the assistance of an expert linguistic opinion that are available on the public record in Australia. Such cases may be resolved privately between parties, or are otherwise not a matter for the courts. An example of the former involves an alleged vodka trademark infringement addressed by Heydon in an unpublished report.

In this case, the party owning the trademark for an existing brand of vodka challenged the right of another vodka manufacturer to register a new vodka brand name on the grounds that the new brand name was so close to the existing (complainant's) brand name, that the two would be easily confused, especially in the noisy environment of a licensed premises. Heydon's opinion was sought by the complainants to explore whether there was a case to be made based on the likely pronunciation of each brand name by Australian speakers and whether the perception of each name by Australian hearers was likely to be similar enough to cause confusion. The analysis therefore involved Australian variational sociolinguistics and phonemics. As the case was resolved privately, no legal precedent was set for the involvement of a linguist in such a case.

In a trademark dispute that did appear before the courts, *N. V. Sumatra Tobacco Trading Company v British American Tobacco Services Limited* 2011, John Hajek, a linguist at the University of Melbourne, gave evidence in relation to the similarity of the two brand names and the capacity of the target market of consumers to distinguish between them. His evidence and his expertise were explicitly recognised by the court in relation to 'opinions about language structure and grammatical and syntactic analysis', but the analysis of language *use* was excluded. The judge in that case expressed his opinion that the scope of linguistic expertise does not include sociolinguistic analysis of likely pronunciation of a word or phrase or 'the propensity of consumers to abbreviate Lucky Dream and Lucky Draw in the way he [Hajek] suggests is authoritative'. Thus, the decision appears to demonstrate how legal professionals, including judges, can hold certain beliefs about what a linguist can examine as part of their analysis.

> However, I accept that as an expert in linguistics, Professor Hajek is in a position to express opinions about language structure and grammatical and syntactic analysis. However, on the question of the disposition of market participants engaged in consumer transactions in relation to particular goods in a particular environment within the context of particular behavioural experience all conditioned by a particular regulatory environment, I am not persuaded that Professor Hajek's predictive opinion about the propensity of consumers to abbreviate Lucky Dream and Lucky Draw in the way he suggests is authoritative in terms of the field of his expertise. (paragraph 284)

Felicity Cox has given linguistic evidence in several trademark disputes over pronunciation of similar-sounding product names. The judge's comments on her evidence in one of these cases suggested that while the evidence relating to phonetics and phonology was scientific, it was not immediately relevant to the case material because 'it has no contextual application to the engaged field of common human endeavour' (*JBS Australia Pty Ltd v Australian Meat Group Pty Ltd* 2017, paragraph 271). This appears to be based on a misunderstanding about phonology in particular, and the context-dependent nature of phonological analysis.

Whereas the decisions in these cases acknowledge the expertise of the linguists in relation to the systematic analysis of linguistic structures, they do not seem to give due recognition to the capacity for linguists to comment on the interpretation of language in context.

Metaphor, Hyperbole and Literal Interpretation

In a case which goes to the heart of the referential language ideology, Kate Burridge gave expert evidence in the Western Australian State Administrative Tribunal in the *Medical Board of Australia v Roberts* 2014. Dr Roberts was a renowned paediatrician accused of professional misconduct, based on notes he had written to the parents of twin nine-year-old boys. Burridge's report was about the use of metaphor and hyperbole in a note to the mother which included 'I recommend to your husband that he beat (physically) each and any of you our sons (*sic*) who swear and offend his wife (that is Mother) . . . to within in (*sic*) an inch of his life'. Despite Burridge's cross-examination being focused on the dictionary meaning of words, the judge agreed with her that 'it is difficult to conceive how any reasonable reader of those words might interpret them literally'. The judge 'nonetheless consider[ed] that a reasonable reader would construe those words as a recommendation to effect corporal punishment to a degree beyond what . . . could be referred to as "non-abusive smacking"' (paragraph 152), and Dr Roberts was found guilty of the lesser charge of unprofessional conduct.

Lexical Meaning in a Language Other than English

Expert linguistic evidence is sometimes sought for the meaning of a word or phrase from a language other than English.

Helen Harper gave evidence in a 1995 case about a speaker of Torres Strait Creole (to be discussed in Section 3.6.1), part of which explained possible linguistic interference from the accused's first language in the statement to police that she had wanted to 'kill' the victim. The word 'kill' is ambiguous in this creole language and can be used to mean 'kill' in the English sense, or alternatively 'hurt' or 'maim'. Bruce Rigsby had given similar evidence about the lexical item 'kill' in the case of another Torres Strait Creole speaker in the late 1970s (Eades, 1994).

In a 2015 Victorian County Court case, Ikuko Nakane gave expert evidence which focused on the analysis of a Japanese expression that has multiple meanings, which had been used in the notebook of a defendant. And in a 2021 appeal case in Japan, she prepared an expert report about meanings of two everyday Japanese expressions in an earlier judgment.

3.5.2 Other Applied Linguistic Work on Legal Language

As indicated in the introduction to Section 3.5, Australia is recognised internationally in the plain language and law movement, especially through the work of Australian linguist and Professor of English, the late Robert Eagleson, beginning in the 1970s. He was instrumental in the creation of the NRMA Plain English Insurance Policy in 1976. Eagleson's ground-breaking report for the Law Reform Commission of Victoria (1987), *Plain English and the Law*, was republished online by the Victorian Law Reform Commission (2017) (see also Eagleson, 1990). In 1990 Eagleson co-founded with Peter Butt the Law Foundation Centre for Plain Legal Language at the University of Sydney.

John Gibbons (1990, 2001) worked with New South Wales police on simplifying the language of the police caution, and his report on this project shows that not all of his suggestions were adopted (Gibbons, 1990, 2001; see also Rock, 2007: 259 for a similar example from England and Wales). More recently, Gibbons has worked with the Victorian Charge Book Committee on making Jury Instructions more comprehensible. This work highlights the ongoing tension that arises from the two-audience problem of legal language (Gibbons, 2003). Gibbons argues that it is important 'not to sacrifice comprehension by the primary audience [here, the jury] for the sake of the secondary audience – an appeal court' (2017: 144). With this approach, his analysis of linguistic and comprehension issues in jury instructions led to his suggestion for a 'radical recasting' of the wording of instructions rather than revising them 'at a superficial linguistic level' (2017: 159). But his suggestions for revision were not adopted by the committee.

Plain English is especially important in situations involving speakers of English as an additional language. In the last decade a number of linguists have worked with lawyers and legal organisations on improving access to justice through projects aimed at making legal language more comprehensible. These projects highlight ways in which the monolingual language ideology (Section 2.3.3) is being addressed, and show that linguists are making a significant and substantial contribution to such work.

The most accessible and extensive example is the *Plain English Legal Dictionary: Northern Territory Criminal Law*, jointly published by the independent Aboriginal research agency ARDS, the independent Aboriginal legal service NAAJA and the Northern Territory Government's Aboriginal Interpreter Service AIS (Aboriginal Resource and Development Services et al., 2015). This dictionary takes a story-based approach to the collation of legal definitions in plain language into simple narratives showing common usage of these terms. More than 300 definitions are also provided in a regular, dictionary-style list. The main purpose of the dictionary is to improve access to justice for speakers of Australian Indigenous languages and speakers of Australian Aboriginal English. One of the challenges for the dictionary team is that many Anglo legal terms (e.g. 'bail', 'arrest' or 'warrant') have no direct equivalent in Indigenous languages, which are part of the oldest living culture in the world and do not include ways of expressing English settler legal concepts (see also Section 5).

A crucial part of the four-year preparation of the dictionary was the translation of legal terms into plain English before translation into Djambarrpuyngu (the main dialect of Yolngu Matha, a widely spoken Aboriginal language in the Northern Territory). Reiterative drafting was required between legal English, plain English and Djambarrpuyngu. The resulting *Plain English Dictionary*

(ARDS et al., 2015) and *Djambarrpuyngu Dictionary* (ARDS, 2015) were the product of intensive collaboration between Aboriginal interpreters, and lawyers and linguists (including lawyer-linguist Ben Grimes and linguists Steve Swartz, Howard Amery and Marilyn McLellan).

The Northern Territory has also been leading the country in the preparation in languages other than English of recordings of suspects' rights in police interviews (known as the caution). This began in the late 1990s with work by linguist Michael Cooke and lawyer Jenny Hardy to produce a plain English version, then approved by the Departments of the Attorney-General and the Office of the Director of Public Prosecutions, as well as police and representative lawyers. This 'front translation' (Bowen, 2021b: 322) was then translated into fifteen Aboriginal languages. The resulting audio-recordings, intended as a resource for police, are described as 'preambles' to the caution (Mildren, 1999), providing explanation, rather than being limited to direct translation (Section 5.1; Bowen, 2021b). There is no public information about the extent to which these recordings were used.

In 2015, the Northern Territory Aboriginal Interpreter Service completed a similar project, in order to provide much shorter versions, again working from a plain English front translation. Audiovisual recordings were produced in eighteen Aboriginal languages of suspects' right to silence and their right to inform a person of their location: https://cmc.nt.gov.au/aboriginal-affairs/aborigi nal-interpreter-service/aboriginal-language-police-cautions-aboriginal-inter preter-service. Lawyer-linguist Ben Grimes was part of the multi-disciplinary group comprising interpreters, linguists, police officers and lawyers. Again, it has not been possible to ascertain the extent to which these recordings are used. See Section 5.1 for Bowen's (2021b) discussion of the complex issues involved in these 'intercultural translation[s] of vague legal language' (p. 308).

A similar project in Western Australia was part of the police response to the decision in the *Gibson* case, to be discussed in Section 3.6.1. The 'Yarning' app, on the phones of all police officers, delivers information, in plain English and eight Aboriginal languages, about the right of suspects in police custody to contact a lawyer or family member. The app helps police identify a suspect's strongest language, and it also provides a quick link to Aboriginal Interpreting Western Australia (AIWA) who worked with police to develop the app (Bowen, 2021c). Lawyer-linguist Alex Bowen was part of AIWA's team for this project.

A different approach to plain English in the law, with which lawyer-linguist Ben Grimes has been involved, is the Blurred Borders Resource kit. This is a legal communication tool used by frontline service providers working with Aboriginal clients in regional and remote locations of Western Australia and the Northern Territory. Focusing on the key legal concepts around bail and the criminal process, and family violence and child protection, this kit uses visual art, plain language and storytelling to explain legal concepts and processes, https://blurredborders.legalaid.wa.gov.au/about-blurred-borders.

Leading Australian lexicographer Pam Peters has developed a free online dictionary of 350 words and phrases (known as a 'term bank') used in Australia Family Law and mediation services. Commissioned by the Federal Attorney-General's Department, the TermFinder™ term bank in family law has also been translated into eight community languages, namely Arabic, Chinese (Modern), Chinese (Traditional), Filipino, Korean, Spanish, Turkish and Vietnamese: https://lawtermfinder.mq.edu.au/.

A pilot Indigenous family law term bank in Easy English has also been created, which provides visual support, and is organised by related concepts, rather than alphabetically, partly using resources from the Blurred Borders project (see above). https://lawtermfinder.mq.edu.au/easy-read-home.php. There are plans to extend the current 150-word term bank, and to provide audio-recordings of all the verbal material. As with the *Plain English Criminal Law Dictionary*, and the Blurred Borders project, an initiative to help Indigenous people understand the law has the potential to also explain the law to a wide range of other linguistically and culturally diverse people, as well as people with cognitive disabilities.

Attention to legal language is also one of the characteristics of the Law Society of the Northern Territory's (2015) *Indigenous Protocols for Lawyers*, an initiative by lawyers and for lawyers, which seeks to codify knowledge from applied linguistics and language work into recommendations and guidelines. One of the six Protocols is 'Use "plain English" to the greatest extent possible'. The publication's five-page explanation and exemplification of how to do this has been adopted in several other publications for lawyers and courts, including JCCD (2022) and Law Society of South Australia (2020). Lawyer-linguist Ben Grimes was actively involved in the writing of this document.

Finally, the *Guidelines for Communicating Rights to Non-Native Speakers of English in Australia, England and Wales, and the USA*, www.aaal.org/guide lines-for-communication-rights, produced by the Communication of Rights Group (CoRG, 2015), comprised seven Australian forensic linguists as part of the group of 21 linguists, lawyers, psychologists and interpreters: Michael Cooke, Diana Eades (co-convenor), John Gibbons, Ben Grimes, Sandra Hale, David Moore and Ikuko Nakane. The focus of CoRG was the communication of rights to non-native speakers in police interviews with suspects, and the intention was to 'translate' research on this topic for practitioners and policy makers. Drawing on linguistic and psychological research, as well as the collective experience of working with specific cases, this Communication of Rights

Group produced a 2000-word guidelines document setting out seven recommendations, as well as providing an explanation intended to be accessible for police officers, lawyers, judges and justice administrators. The document's Appendix is a bibliography of relevant research (Eades & Pavlenko, 2016).

While these positive developments in the use of plain, or clear, English cannot be disputed, the CoRG (2015) Guidelines point out that 'there is no one formulation of rights/cautions that would be immediately understandable to all'. In his work on translations of the right to silence in the Northern Territory, Bowen (2019, 2021a, 2021b) goes further, showing how linguistic work on the wording of legal language is not enough when there are gaps in contextual knowledge about the culture of the law (see Section 5.1).

3.5.3 Research

Australian research on the language of the legal process has paid less attention to the structural aspects of the language of law than the pragmatic aspects (Section 4). But some linguistic research has addressed discourse structure and semantics.

Yon Maley (1994) used a systemic functional linguistics approach to overview the three legal discourses of legislation, trial proceedings and judicial judgments. Her conclusion, in the early years of linguistic research in the law, that reform of legal language is limited by institutional structures, practices and ideologies, resonates with contemporary linguistic concerns about the limits of intercultural translation (e.g. Bowen, Section 5.1).

Three Australian linguists have researched the use of a particular semantic theory (Natural Semantic Metalanguage) in exploring and explaining meaning in law: Cliff Goddard with the words 'enterprise', 'reckless' and 'sudden' (1996); lawyer-linguist Ian Langford (2000) with a focus on the legal terms 'murder', 'manslaughter' and 'homicide'; and Anna Wierzbicka (2003) on the legal terms 'reasonable man' and 'beyond reasonable doubt'.

Heydon (2005) analysed the use of legal terminology in police interviews by applying Conversation Analysis and interactional sociolinguistics to recordings of police interviews from Victoria. She found that the word 'charge', that has a common meaning of 'payment owing', is easily confused for the legal meaning of 'charge', meaning that a person is identified by police as accused of committing an offence, particularly, as in the case described, when the charge is for 'damage to the door'. This use of 'legal homonyms' (Tiersma, 2000) occurs regularly in police interview data, and the impact on laypeople noted by Heydon (2005) is similar to the concerns raised in relation to legal language for partial speakers of English in research (Aboriginal Resource and Development Services, 2008).

3.6 Linguistic Repertoires and Language Diversity

The focus in this section is on the impact of Australia's linguistic diversity on the legal process. The section is structured in terms of the linguistic resources of second language and second dialect speakers of English, sign language users and children. Linguistic resources refers to 'the complex of linguistic means and communicative skills, ... including ... proficiency in, or choice of, a particular language variety' (sometimes termed linguistic repertoire, and referred to by Blommaert (2005: 58) as a 'forgotten context'). The linguistic resources of lay participants in the law have been the focus of much research, expert evidence and practical applications for two decades in Australia. Indeed, forensic linguists here have probably paid more attention to issues which arise from the country's linguistic diversity than forensic linguists in any other country. Several forensic linguists have addressed the monolingual and referential language ideologies introduced in Section 2.3.

3.6.1 Second Language Speakers: Expert Evidence

After Strehlow's 1959 evidence in the *Stuart* case (Section 1.3.1), the earliest expert linguistic evidence involving languages other than English was presented by John Gibbons in several cases in the 1980s and 1990s, before the introduction of audio-recording of police interviews with suspects (Section 1.2.2). Gibbons used findings from research on second language acquisition and language testing in answering questions about the accuracy of alleged confessions which non-native speakers had claimed were fabricated (Gibbons, 1990, 1995; see also Jensen, 1995; Eades, 1993 for a second dialect speaker).

Over a period of more than two decades, several linguists have written expert reports, and in some cases given expert evidence, concerning linguistic resources of individual non-native speakers of English, typically addressing the question of whether a defendant could have understood their right to silence, and/or particular questions, in a police interview. The monolingual language ideology (Section 2.3.3) is at the heart of these cases (as indicated by both discussions with the linguists named below and the publications referred to). Linguists often report the need to address the lack of awareness in the law that even if speakers of English as an additional language can conduct a basic conversation in English, they may nevertheless need an interpreter for more complex interactions such as a police interview (see also Section 3.6.3).

There is no way of knowing how many linguists have provided such expertise, but we are aware that a list would include the following, some of whom have published in the linguistics or law field, drawing on a specific case in which they have presented expert evidence: Denise Angelo, Alex Bowen, Michael Cooke (e.g. 1996), Maria Doyle, Diana Eades (e.g. 2018), Cathie Elder, Rod Gardner, John Gibbons (e.g. 1990, 1995), Helen Harper, David Ingram, John Ingram, Marie-Thérèse Jensen (1995), Ute Knoch, Ian Malcolm, Prudy McLaughlin, David Moore, Ikuko Nakane and Carmel O'Shannessy.

Several of these cases, and much of the research discussed in this section, have involved Aboriginal second language speakers of English. In contrast, very little work has dealt with the other group of Indigenous Australians, namely Torres Strait Islanders. However, in an unreported 1995 case in north Queensland, Helen Harper gave expert linguistic evidence about the police interview of a Torres Strait Creole speaker charged with attempted murder (*R v Izumi* 1995).

Part of Harper's evidence was that the accused had not properly understood the police caution or a number of the questions she was asked by police (see also Section 3.5.1). Two of the main issues in Harper's linguistic evidence were (i) that Torres Strait Creole is not the same as English, and (ii) that there was no evidence that Ms Izumi had understood the caution. The judge accepted Harper's evidence and decided to exclude the police interview evidence. The murder charge was dropped, and Mrs Izumi pleaded guilty to unlawful wounding (Tresize, 1996).

In *WA v Gibson* 2014, a Western Australian Supreme Court judge made important rulings about language proficiency and the need for an interpreter, in a refreshing departure from the referentialist and monolingual ideologies so frequently seen in the law (Section 2.3). Mr Gibson is a speaker of three Aboriginal languages and a partial speaker of English (Section 3.6.3). The judge refused to accept that his 'yes' answers in a police interview to 'do you understand?' questions were indications of understanding (referring to the expert linguistic evidence provided by Eades, as well as David Ingram and Maria Doyle; see Eades, 2018). Instead, the judge pointed to problems with the 'assumption that the answers given always reflect an understanding of the questions asked' (paragraph 74). Not only did the judge reject the idea that the meaning of the answer 'yes' was fixed, he also made it clear that linguistic and cultural contexts were central to meaning and to his decision in the case: particularly Mr Gibson's very low English proficiency and the pressure in his first language (from an older male relative to whom he owed respect) that directly contradicted what the police were saying to him in his third language.

3.6.2 Languages Other than English: Research on Interpreting

In Australia more than 300 languages other than English are spoken, and 21 per cent of Australians speak a language other than English at home. The conservative and traditionally Anglocentric institution of the law has come a long way in the last fifty years in recognising the importance of interpreting, but linguistic research, casework and interactions with legal professionals and law enforcement show that the monolingual language ideology (Section 2.3.3) continues to influence policy and practice.

For example, the law's assumption that monolingualism is, and should be, the norm can give rise to objections about a second language speaker's request for an interpreter, as indicated above. Such objections can be seen in terms of a common misconception among legal professionals that if such a person can converse in English at a conversational level, then they do not need an interpreter, and even that they should not have an interpreter in legal interviews (Section 3.6.3; Eades, 2018). However, research on the language of bilingual people in a range of countries and social contexts shows that it is common for people to have much less proficiency in their second language than their first language.

Frequent misconceptions about the nature of bilingual language use can sometimes result in situations where people with some bilingual fluency are expected to act as if they are monolingual speakers of their language other than English. In courts, witnesses who do not hide the fact that they have some bilingual fluency can run the risk of being seen as misrepresenting their need for an interpreter. Thus, in order to deal with complex questions with an interpreter, they are expected to ignore the simple English questions (for which they may not need interpreting assistance), as the court expects them to act as monolingual speakers of their first language. In legal situations which do not adhere to this aspect of the monolingual language ideology, the rights to justice of bilingual people may sometimes be better served, as Cooke (1996) illustrates with an example of a Djambarrpuynyngu and English-speaking defendant from northern Australia (*R v M* 1995).

The most prolific Australian linguistic researcher on issues impacting users of languages other than English in the law is Sandra Hale, whose contributions are recognised not just within Australia, but internationally, since her 2004 study of court interpreting in trials involving Spanish interpreters. Hale's micro-analysis of lawyers' discourse markers and question types in interpreted proceedings shows how and why it is so difficult for interpreters to achieve one of the central goals of interpreting, namely pragmatic accuracy (that is, conveying speaker meaning, such as sarcasm, surprise and disbelief, as well as utterance meaning).

Since this seminal study, Hale and her colleagues have continued to research a wide range of aspects of legal interpreting, including issues of quality, codes of ethics, role expectations, the impact of interpreters on legal proceedings, the perceptions of interpreters held by service providers and non-English speakers, and the impact of working conditions on interpreter performance (e.g. Hale & Stern, 2011; Hale, 2013). The findings of this research directly impact the training and certification of interpreters, areas of professional practice in which Hale is arguably the national leader. At the same time Hale has played a key role in the education of legal professionals, including judicial officers, about what is involved in interpreting and how they can work with interpreters in the delivery of justice.

Using a combination of experimental and discourse analytical methods, Hale's most recent research has focused on different aspects of police and court interpreting, including the effect on interpreter performance of interpreter education and background (Hale, Goodman-Delahunty & Martschuk, 2019), language combination, interpreter mode (Hale et al., 2017) and interpreter presence or remoteness – e.g. via videolink– (Hale et al., 2022). Interpreters' maintenance of strategic investigative interview techniques, including rapport building, as well as their interpretation of vulgar and emotional language has also been a key area of investigation (Hale et al., 2020; see also Lai & Mulayim, 2014; Mulayim, Lai & Norma, 2015).

In all of her work Hale counters widespread misconceptions within the law of what it means to speak English as an additional language, especially the language ideologies of referentialism, monolingualism and communication as coded message transfer (Section 2.3). Consistent with these assumptions about language is the widespread misconception among legal professionals that interpreters can, and should, act as a language 'machine' or conduit (Section 2.3.3.; see also Smith-Khan, 2017).

Hale's direct input was crucial to the publication of the *Recommended National Standards for Working with Interpreters in Courts and Tribunals* (JCCD, 2022; and see Section 2.3.3). Throughout this document, accurate interpreting is defined, following the AUSIT Code of Ethics (AUSIT, 2012), as

> the optimal and complete transfer of the meaning of the other language into English and of English into the other language, preserving the **content and intent** of the other language or English (as the case may be) without omission or distortion. (JCCD, 2022: 23, emphasis added)

This important document makes it clear that the job of interpreting is to transfer both semantic and pragmatic meaning, that is referential meaning and speaker's meaning in the context of their talk.

While most of Hale's research on the actual process of legal interpreting has focused on pragmatic challenges in court contexts, a number of other linguists have examined other kinds of linguistic challenges for legal interpreting, or for lay participants in legal processes who speak English as an additional language but do not have full proficiency in English.

Ludmila Stern (e.g. 2001) examines linguistic and cross-cultural challenges in the three war crimes prosecutions and the trial held in Australia in the late 1980s to early 1990s, when several Ukrainian people were brought to Australia as witnesses to crimes allegedly committed during the second world war. She compares these challenges and related interpreting issues with trials in the International Criminal Tribunal for the Former Yugoslavia in The Hague. Jieun Lee (e.g. 2009) highlights linguistic differences between the Korean and English languages in the expression of definiteness in noun phrases, presenting a compelling example which highlights the importance of interpreters being seen as language professionals who may sometimes need to explain linguistic challenges to the court.

While most research on interpreters and second language speakers in the legal system has focused on courtroom hearings, Nakane has examined interpreted police interviews, using a discourse pragmatic framework (e.g. 2007, 2014). The catalyst for this research was her analysis of a police interview in a 2002 Federal Court case, and her expert report for an Individual Communication submitted to the United Nations Human Rights Commission in 2005, concerning a 1994 Victorian County Court case. Nakane's work highlights the impact of interpreters on the interactional dynamics of police interviews, as interviewer and interviewee negotiate over the construction of competing stories.

Macfarlane et al. (2019) take a critical lens to the institutional management of interpreters in police interviews and courts in Australia. The authors note that a failure to address shortfalls in the provision of a professional interpreter service reflects the institutional racism in Australia's legal system whereby English proficiency is privileged and overrides the preferences of clients who speak other languages, including Aboriginal languages. Despite Lo Bianco's (1987) optimism about a shift away from entrenched English monolingualism, this work finds that 'while the country might claim to tolerate limited amounts of linguistic diversity in private circles, efforts to enforce linguistic unification through English remain structurally embedded, especially in public domains' (p. 52).

A somewhat different issue concerning interpreters in the legal process is the wide-ranging Australian linguistic research concerning interpreters for deaf jurors. This research is leading the way internationally in investigating whether the exclusion of deaf people from juries, common in many countries, is justified by the reasons advanced within the law.

More than fifteen years ago three Macquarie University researchers began investigating this issue (linguist Jemina Napier, lawyer David Spencer and interpreter-linguist David Sabolcec), producing a report for the New South Wales Law Reform Commission (Napier, Spencer & Sabolcec, 2007). Since then, linguists Napier and Hale, and lawyers Spencer and Mehera San Roque, have conducted research including studies which reveal that there is no difference in the ability of hearing jurors and deaf jurors (with interpreters) to understand judges' directions and summations to the jury. One of the other studies in the project surveyed legal professionals and sign language interpreters in seven countries about their perceptions of the impact of a deaf person (receiving the evidence and participating in jury deliberations with the assistance of an interpreter) on the jury and on the outcome of trials. This study was further enriched by focus group research with stakeholders. The final study (e.g. Hale et al., 2017; Napier et al., 2019) was based on a mock trial involving eight legal professionals, two deaf jurors and two professionally qualified sign language interpreters.

The conclusion of this multi-faceted research programme is that 'deaf people can comprehend legal discourse found in the judicial system and that their presence in the court and jury rooms is not detrimental to the delivery of a fair trial to the accused' (Napier et al. 2019: 263). In addition, the research highlighted the 'substantive and logistical hurdles' that need to be overcome for deaf people to serve on juries, and suggests education programmes and 'systematic changes in the legal system' (Napier et al. 2019: 263, see also Hale et al., 2017).

A hallmark of this research is the involvement of lawyers and linguists in the research teams and the inclusion in its many stages of legal professionals, interpreters and deaf people. Some parallels can be noted with the way in which linguists have worked with legal professionals and Aboriginal interpreters to address problems arising from legal language for Aboriginal second language speakers of English in the Northern Territory and Western Australia (Section 3.6.3). And as with this latter work, the research on deaf jurors is creating change within the legal system. Australian Human Rights organisation Remedy Australia (2021) shows 'Australia is on the cusp of making its juries more inclusive for people with hearing and vision disabilities' (p 19), with the Australian Capital Territory leading the way with legislative reform.

3.6.3 Aboriginal and Torres Strait Islander Second Language Speakers specifically

The specific linguistic contexts for speakers of Aboriginal languages in the legal process have been written about by linguists since the late 1970s (e.g. Brennan 1979; Nash, 1979; McKay, 1985). Michael Walsh is one of the linguists who has published on linguistic (and interactional) issues involved in taking evidence from Aboriginal people in land claims and native title proceedings (at both tribunals and trials). Harold Koch (1985) analysed linguistic features ('pronunciation, vocabulary and grammar') of the non-standard English of Aboriginal claimants which lead to miscommunication during the preparation of land claims and tribunal hearings.

Michael Cooke's research in remote Arnhem Land since the 1990s (e.g. 1995a, 1995b, 1996) provides the most detailed examination of miscommunication with Aboriginal speakers of traditional languages in the legal process. His work, as well as David Moore's (e.g. 2022), with speakers of Aboriginal languages, adds to that by Hale and others discussed in Section 3.6.2 on interpreting for speakers of immigrant languages.

However, in contrast to most of the Australian research with non-native-speaking immigrants, most of the research and expert evidence with Aboriginal people who are non-native speakers of English focuses on legal processes where interpreting has not been provided, because participants (whether lay participants and/or legal professionals) assume that English will work. There are difficulties in theory and in practice with deciding when an interpreter is required to communicate adequately with an Aboriginal person in a legal context (Law Society of the Northern Territory, 2015; Cooke, 2002).

Cooke's work (see references above, and 2002, 2004, 2009) has highlighted the linguistic reality that many Aboriginal people from remote communities are partial speakers of English as a second (or subsequent) language, with their capacity to communicate in standard English compromised because of interference from their Aboriginal language(s), at all levels from pronunciation to pragmatics. Frequent and often unrecognised miscommunication commonly results, particularly at lower levels of English proficiency (Cooke, 2002: 8–11).

Cooke's contributions include his 1996 case study (see Section 3.6.2) which highlights the importance of stand-by interpreting in court for witnesses (including defendants) who have sufficient proficiency in English to answer simple biographical and narrative questions, but whose proficiency is not sufficient to talk about more complex issues such as explaining their state of mind. Cooke has also provided expert evidence in cases in NT and Western Australia, and has made a major contribution to the application of linguistics in the training and accrediting of interpreters over several decades.

Cooke (2002), Nick Evans (2002) and Bowen (2019) have also shown some specific linguistic challenges for Aboriginal partial speakers of English in police interviews, courtroom hearings and land claim hearings which relate to the mismatch between specific English modal verbs ('have to', 'should' and 'can') and the expression of modality in Aboriginal languages. While this might appear to be a small area of linguistic difference in the resources of people communicating in English in legal contexts, the work of these scholars reveals the important consequences for justice. It also highlights the widespread impact of the lack of understanding of the need for interpreters that results from the monolingual language ideology (Section 2.3.3).

Linguists working with second language speakers of Aboriginal languages in the law have not restricted their attention to the linguistic context that is the focus of this section. See Sections 4 and 5 for studies and applications that focus on interactional and sociocultural contexts.

3.6.4 Second Dialect Speakers: Aboriginal People

Some attention has also been focused on linguistic issues impacting people who speak Aboriginal English as their main language, for example in relation to miscommunication that can arise from dialectal differences in word choice and meaning (e.g. Eades, 2010: 173–5). For research and expert evidence about differences in language use and sociocultural context for Aboriginal speakers of varieties of English, see Sections 4.2.2, 4.2.3 and 5.

3.6.5 Developmental Issues: Child Witnesses

Finally in this consideration of linguistic resources, research by Brennan and Brennan (1988; see also Brennan 1995) addresses the consequences of ignoring the developmental linguistic proficiency of young children when they are questioned in court. Their study first categorised thirteen linguistic features of complex or confusing questions asked of child witnesses. They then tested thirty school children on the comprehensibility of questions asked by lawyers, compared to those asked by teachers and counsellors. The study found that the children were unable to adequately understand 85 per cent of the lawyer questions, while almost all of the counsellor questions and most of the teacher questions were understood most of the time.

Heydon (1998, 2005: 148–64, 2008a) and La Rooy et al. (2015) have examined the language of questions used in interviews with children by police. This work has added important nuance to the literature on child interviewing, such as further specification of appropriate question types beyond the usual 'open vs closed' typology.

Pamela Snow has contributed research on narratives used by young speakers that supports speech pathologists in working with children and young people in detention, and in other institutional justice settings (e.g. Snow & Powell, 2005).

In the thirty-five years since Brennan's study, the law has taken many steps to address a range of issues (not limited to linguistic issues) impacting legal interviews with children. This work includes pre-recording the direct evidence of child witnesses for the trial in a less intimidating environment than the courtroom and reducing the time the child needs to spend answering questions in court. A recent initiative is the provision of a 'Children's Champion' (or 'Witness Intermediary') to assess communication needs of child witnesses and to inform police and the court of the best ways to communicate with the child giving evidence.

3.7 Laws about Language

With the growing involvement of lawyers in forensic linguistics, two people have focused attention on laws about language.

Lawyer Elyse Methven (e.g. 2018) uses Critical Discourse Analysis in her transdisciplinary study of the law's treatment of 'offensive language', and particularly discursive constructions within the law of swearing at police.

Lawyer-linguist Alexandra Grey brings legal scholarship to the issue of language rights, with her study of laws, policies and practices relating to minority language rights in China (2021). Within Australia, Grey's examination of language rights includes her examination, with linguist Alyssa Severin, of government communication with linguistically diverse communities (Grey & Severin, 2022).

4 Interactional Contexts

Australian sociolinguists have investigated language in the law with a focus on the interactional contexts of the language data being analysed, primarily in three main legal contexts – investigative interviews, courtroom hearings and refugee status determination interviews and related tribunal/courtroom hearings – in all of which interviewing is the central approach.

In this section we discuss linguistic attention to interaction in legal settings that has not already been covered in Section 3.6, under Linguistic Resources, where much of the work on linguistic contexts also deals with interactional contexts.

4.1 Investigative Interviewing

4.1.1 Interactional Structures in Investigative Interviews

Linguistic contributions to the work of police investigators and other forms of investigative process in the Australian justice environment have focused on the interactional structures of interviews and how such structures affect the information that is provided by the lay participants in legal settings. Police investigative interviews form the basis for information gathering in many criminal justice cases. Such interviews are conducted according to regulations, which are explained in police training manuals, written to ensure that police interviewing procedures comply with the relevant state and federal legislation.

However, beyond the specific requirements of the legislation, which focuses on legal rights and points of proof, police are trained in strategies of questioning and conversational management techniques. Linguistic research has identified the impact of various question types on the informativeness of the response, and the extent to which turn-taking strategies can affect the cooperation of the interviewee – an interactional version of rapport building.

The capacity for interviewees in various legal contexts to provide their own version of events is explored through Goffman's participation roles, as well as conversation analysis and topic management (Heydon, 2019). The linguistic analysis of the interactional context in the justice system provides insights that complement other forms of analysis, mainly psychology (Heydon, 2019). For instance, psychologists have identified the ways that an eyewitness's brain stores the memory of an event, and the cognitive factors that can affect recall (Milne & Bull, 1999), whereas linguistic analysis can identify the most appropriate conversational strategies to maximise the opportunities for that recall to be expressed verbally in response to a question or prompt (Heydon, 2012).

The nature of the work by Australian linguists on police interviewing has been significant in its consideration of current police training methods and strategies employed by officers when conducting interviews to maximise the evidentiary value of the information provided by the interviewee. Thus, the institutional setting has been important to the examination of the interactional contexts of police interviewing.

The interactional and institutional contexts can also affect the gathering of information in a written format. Research into the interactional features of written forms to collect reports of sexual assault as an alternative or precursor to a formal police interview is being led by an Australian research team with a linguistic focus.

Again, the intertwining of institutional and interactional contexts for forensic linguistic research has led to innovative work on the nature of narratives submitted as part of an online account of sexual violence and the impact on policing and justice outcomes for stakeholders (Heydon & Powell, 2018).

The multilingual context of legal interactions in Australia has provided a wealth of opportunities for the exploration of interpreter-mediated communications. Cross-cultural communication as well as pragmatic analysis of interpreted police interviews has contributed substantially to the field internationally. For instance, Miranda Lai's work on the relationship between cognitive interviewing strategies and interpreted interviewing was the first of its kind (Heydon & Lai, 2013; Lai & Mulayim, 2014; Mulayim, Lai & Norma, 2015) and has gained traction internationally, especially amongst practitioners. For example, the FBI and the High Value Detainee Interrogation Group were specifically interested in the work of Australian linguists (including Heydon) in 2013 because of the unique findings that Australian researchers had generated in relation to police interviewing in multilingual contexts.

4.1.2 Lie Detection

As discussed above, the focus of police interviewing in Australia has followed professional practice in the UK and New Zealand, which emphasises the elicitation of a free narrative as the most reliable form of information gathering. There is a further benefit to this narrative-based approach to police interviewing, and other forms of legal information gathering, which is its role in deception detection.

Credibility assessment is a common aspect of proceedings in courtrooms in Australia and around the world. The right to a fair trial rests in part on the principle that a person who is accused of, or witness to, a crime must be given the opportunity to give their evidence in person where their 'credibility' can be assessed by the judge and/or jury. This is a complex area of jurisprudence, but underlying the notion of credibility is a belief that live, spoken interaction can provide an opportunity for a hearer to assess the truthfulness, or credibility, of the speaker, based on the hearer's perception of the speaker's demeanour, absent any relevant factual evidence (Porter & Ten Brinke, 2009: 120). This reliance on hearer perception is challenged by research, which demonstrates that indicators of truthfulness commonly used in such situations (eye contact, fidgeting, hesitant speech) are culturally bound, or equally associated with nervousness, and do not stand up to scientific testing (e.g. Granhag, Vrij & Verschuere, 2015). Additionally, Australian research has pointed out that factors which have been found to sway a jury's opinion include the performance of a court interpreter, which can be highly prejudicial for witnesses and defendants providing evidence in a language other than English (Hale et al., 2017).

In police investigations, lie detection has largely given way to investigative processes that rely on hard evidence and detailed accounts from suspects or witnesses. However, among the most high-profile consultant investigators engaged by Australian police there are still proponents of scientifically invalid techniques such as statement analysis (searching written statements for 'markers' of deception), polygraph testing and 'micro-expressions', a behavioural analysis technique which sits within the 'body language' category of lie detection (see for instance https://www.stevevanaperen.com/).

As a form of language analysis, the lie detection methods that rely on the examination of written statements for markers of detection have been critiqued in Australia for their lack of an underlying theory of language structure and use. Heydon (2008b, 2019) finds that purported lie detection techniques such as Scientific Content Analysis (SCAN) are not based on sound linguistic theory and are promoted to police as almost magical in their power to uncover deception in a written statement. In a system of interrogation which relies on coercion to elicit confessions, police are more likely to be drawn to anything that can assure them that they are interrogating only the guilty parties. Hence, in the USA where the coercive Reid technique of interviewing is dominant, lie detection courses and techniques find a ready market. In Australian police academies, lie detection has largely been replaced by training that emphasises an investigative approach to interviewing (Adam & van Golde, 2020). However, lie detection proponents still find an audience in Australia amongst other investigative and interview-based professions, such as in the recruitment and security sectors.

Australian police interviewing contexts are dominated by the PEACE model of interviewing, which relies on cognitive psychology for its underpinning conceptual framework and evidence base. The techniques used within this model promote the elicitation of a free narrative, and this provides a better opportunity for lie detection than the aforementioned methods, like SCAN, polygraph testing or micro expression analysis. The reason for this is that a detailed oral account from a suspect, or witness, freely given without leading or suggestive questions is regarded as the most reliable form of evidence. It also maximises the opportunities for detectives to check the interviewee's account against any other evidence gathered in the case. The linguistic analysis of participant roles provides an interactional perspective on the elicitation of information that can separate information that originates from the interviewee's own version of events from information that originates from a police version of events. This could be valuable in the assessment of interviewee credibility when testing the interviewee's version against known facts in the case.

4.2 Courtroom Communication and Beyond

4.2.1 Early Work

The first Australian linguistic publication about language in the courtroom was Eades' (1992) handbook for lawyers, written to dispel widespread myths and ignorance about Aboriginal ways of speaking English, and to suggest ways lawyers could engage in more effective communication with Aboriginal clients and witnesses.

This publication was partly motivated by judicial reactions to Eades' expert linguistic evidence in the appeal in *R v Condren* 1987 (Section 1.3.2). The evidence was about the striking differences in an alleged confession to police between the words attributed to an Aboriginal man charged of murder, and his dialect of Aboriginal English. The linguistic evidence was not accepted by the court, whose reasons included biological determinism as an explanation for language usage (in effect, that the Aboriginal man's mother was not dark-skinned enough, *R v Condren* 1987: 275), as well as linguistically uninformed views about language variation.

The earliest linguistic research on courtroom interactions (Walsh, 1994) arose from Michael Walsh's fieldwork in several Aboriginal communities, mostly in remote areas of northern Australia. Walsh found that conversation in these traditionally oriented communities was mostly non-dyadic and continuous, with people often spending time together with the communication channel 'switched on', but including periods of silence, and where talk is not necessarily directed to a particular interlocutor. He showed the contrast with mainstream Australian interactional style, and particularly in the courtroom, where talk is almost always dyadic and non-continuous, and where talk is 'strictly regimented' (p. 226).

4.2.2 Questions and Answers

The central role of the question-answer structure in the courtroom (and through-out the legal process) has been a focus of all the linguistic writing on courtroom language. Luchjenbroers (1997) contributed to the growing international findings about how defendants and witnesses are controlled, coerced and manipulated through the rigid and asymmetrical discourse structure of courtroom hearings, which restricts the interactional rights of witnesses to providing answers to specific questions (see also Gibbons, 2003). Eades (2000) questions the assumption in much of this work that the syntactic form of question types in court has a fixed relationship with the way in which power is exercised, with a study in a NSW court showing how supposedly controlling question types can be taken by witnesses in some hearings as an invitation to explain. And Maley's (2000) analysis of expert witness testimony in a case in the Land and Environment Court makes the case that linguistic analysis needs to include more than 'surface or formal properties' of the talk, such as sentence form or turn-taking.

> In the interpretation of legal language the analyst ... must look to widening discoursal, institutional and cultural contexts and identify the ways in which counsel strive, successfully or otherwise, to establish, negotiate and maintain opposing interpretive frames [throughout different phases of the hearing]. (p. 265)

Eades (e.g. 2000, 2003, 2008b), Walsh (2008) and Cooke (e.g. 1996, 2002) have reported on problems, for Aboriginal witnesses in particular, that arise from the reliance on the question-answer structure.

In Eades' (2000) study, lawyers and judges appear to be overly preoccupied with individual answers to questions rather than the story which a witness is trying to present to the court. The study shows how a focus on answers to questions can prevent lawyers and judges from realising how much they fail to understand about some of the Aboriginal witnesses and their evidence. This lack of understanding resulted, in this New South Wales study, not primarily from linguistic difference, but from differences in sociocultural context (Section 5), compounded by limiting linguistic practices, here courtroom discourse structure.

4.2.3 Assumptions about Storytelling and Retelling

At the centre of courtroom procedure are culturally based assumptions about how witnesses' accounts/stories should be structured, retold and evaluated. Eades' (2008a, 2008b, 2012) in-depth analysis of the cross-examination of three teenage Aboriginal boys in Brisbane Magistrate's Court (*Crawford v Venardos* 1995) is the first Australian linguistic work to come to terms with these assumptions, or language ideologies (see Section 2.3). Her work draws on that of linguistic anthropologists and others in the field of language ideologies in the law (e.g. Matoesian, 2001; Trinch, 2003; Ehrlich, 2012). Eades' study highlights the following assumptions in law concerning verbal interaction, when witness's accounts are told and retold (by themselves and others):

> The ideology of inconsistency (Matoesian, 2001): the assumption that inconsistency between different tellings of a story necessarily indicates lack of truthfulness. This ignores other well-documented reasons for inconsistency, including memory failure and the impact of the interviewer's role in structuring the story.
>
> The ideology of decontextualised fragments: the assumption that individual words or fragments taken from a story can be understood without their context. Focusing on isolated words or phrases without the preceding and following talk, and often by reading from a transcript, with no indication of intonation, pausing, volume etc, can enable a lawyer in cross-examination to convey a rather different version of a witness's earlier story or part(s) of it.
>
> The ideology of repeated questioning: the assumption that repeated questioning provides the opportunity to properly test a witness's truthfulness (see Section 4.1.2). This ignores psycholinguistic research findings about the suggestibility of children in legal interviews, and sociolinguistic research findings about gratuitous concurrence (see Section 5.2).
>
> The ideology of narrator authorship (Trinch, 2003): the assumption that a witness's or interviewee's story is solely their own account. This ignores the interactional context in which the story is narrated, for example how an interviewer's questions shape, frame and even restrict what the witness says.

Eades' micro-analysis of the cross-examination in this case shows the operation of these language ideologies in the courtroom 'business as usual' to legitimise the actions of police removing Aboriginal children from the street (without any evidence of the children's wrongdoing and without charging them with any offence) and abandoning them in the middle of the night in an isolated industrial wasteland. And this language in court is also shown to play a role in reinforcing public discourse about Aboriginal children as a threat to public safety.

These four language ideologies at the heart of the way that laypeople's stories are heard, shaped and assessed in court can be seen as part of the referential ideology introduced in Section 2, that is, the metacommunicative norm that 'we can examine individual utterances out of context' (Ford & Mertz, 2016: 4). They also reveal the assumption that the 'structure of language in court is neutral and reveals the truth' (Ford & Mertz, 2016: 5, drawing on Matoesian, 2016). The referential language ideology is taken up further by Ehrlich and Eades (2016) in their consideration of linguistic and discursive evidence in a range of legal settings, which shows how the law ignores linguistic, situational, interactional and sociocultural context in its determination of questions about consent.

4.2.4 Assessing the Stories of Asylum Seekers

These language ideologies are also an important part of lawyer-linguist Laura Smith-Khan's research on communication with and about asylum seekers, which is resulting in extensive publications in both legal and linguistic journals (e.g. 2017, 2019a, 2019b, 2022). At the heart of the refugee status determination (RSD) process is the asylum seeker's story — of home country, persecution or fear of persecution, often war, and escape. When the veracity of an applicant's story is assessed, by government officials and judicial officers in the tribunal and the court which decide appeals against an initial negative decision, apparent inconsistencies in the applicant's various tellings and retellings of the story become crucial.

Smith-Khan focuses primarily on the analysis of institutional texts, especially on decisions of courts and tribunals which consider asylum interviews (and accompanying application forms and other evidence), as well as published government policy documents which guide the interviews and the RSD process. Her examination (e.g. 2019b) of these institutional texts exposes the monolingual language ideology (Section 2.3.3), for example in expectations that a bilingual person should be fully proficient in both (or all) of the languages they speak. And the four language ideologies from Eades' work outlined above also impact the way that decision-makers assess the witnesses' account. (Unlike approaches used in some criminal investigations which rely on false beliefs about 'markers of deception' (Section 4.1.2), official guidance to the tribunal decision-makers cautions them – but only in general terms – to be aware of 'the effect of cultural differences on demeanour and oral communication' (Smith-Khan, 2019b: 413.)

Building on earlier findings of co-construction of accounts/stories, Smith-Khan shows not only how asylum seekers' stories are constructed, conceptualised, evaluated and contested, but also that credibility itself is also co-constructed, through interviews and policies, in which these problematic assumptions about language play a role. Her most recent work gives reason for optimism that the use of sociolinguistic approaches which limit reliance on problematic language ideologies can lead to the situation where credibility assessments would come to 'play a less prominent role in RSD' and asylum seekers 'would be more likely to be given the benefit of the doubt' (2022: 14).

4.2.5 Other Legal Settings

Australian researchers have also contributed to the small body of linguistic research in alternative legal settings. Candlin and Maley's (1997) analysis of family law mediation sessions found that they combined features of both therapeutic discourse and legal discourse. Zappavigna, Dwyer and Martin (2016; see also Zappavigna & Martin, 2018) conducted ethnographic research on 18 Youth Justice Conferences in Sydney. These conferences are a restorative justice alternative to court for children (under 18) who admit to an offence.

Using functional linguistic and semiotic analysis, they uncover the discursive processes by which interaction in the conferences, strongly directed by the (trained) conference convenors, works to achieve the transformations at the heart of the goals of this form of restorative justice. Their study details convenors 'scaffolding' the negotiation of participants' feelings, and often encouraging participants (including the young offender, the victim and family and support people of each) to 'reframe the matter they are dealing with as an infringement of family, religious, or cultural values, and not simply as a legal violation' (Zappavigna & Martin, 2018: 290). This in-depth linguistic study contributes to the wider sociolegal field by providing the first analysis in the world of the discursive activation of reintegrative shaming, which has been at the heart of the theory of restorative justice.

Stroud (2010) describes processes in the Koori Court in Victoria, an example of an Indigenous sentencing court, where Elders and other respected people from local Indigenous communities sit with the magistrate to talk with defendants who have pleaded guilty, before the magistrate decides on the sentence. As these Indigenous courts are an addition to the sentencing process, they are not bound by rules of evidence, and witnesses speak directly, without lawyers. Defendants' personal, family and social situations are examined in a 'power-sharing' legal context in which local cultural beliefs, lifestyles and practices (including ways of communicating) are recognised as central to the issues which need to be addressed in relation to the offender's actions, relationships and sentencing (see Eades, 2010: 225–8).

Dieckmann and Rojas-Lizana (2016) use discourse analysis to study free legal advice meetings, in particular looking for evidence of possible power imbalance between lawyers and clients. Focusing on the use of legal or formal register and interruptions, they found that the lawyer advice meetings studied are characterised by the 'discourse of facilitation (participatory) rather than of domination (authoritarian) on the part of the lawyer'. Thus, they align more with expert advice-giving sessions than with studies (in other countries) of lawyer-client consultation.

Finally, in addition to her work on Australian police interviews, Ikuko Nakane has been researching the 'hybrid' Japanese courtroom (e.g. Nakane, 2020). Her main focus is the ways in which the combined adversarial and inquisitorial approaches in trials are realised in courtroom discourse.

5 Sociocultural Contexts

Language is always used in a cultural context, and the culture of the law, embedded within mainstream Anglo culture, is a specialised professional culture, which presents differences and challenges for many lay people who participate in the legal process. In sociolinguistic and anthropological linguistic research, expert evidence and applications of linguistics, several Australians have focused attention on this aspect of the context of language in the law. This section is structured in terms of some of the main impacts of sociocultural context on the language data being analysed by forensic linguists.

5.1 Culture of Law(s)

The most striking impact of sociocultural context on language in the law is seen in situations involving the participation of Aboriginal people. While many non-Aboriginal people within the western law are unaware of Aboriginal law, Aboriginal scholars are increasingly drawing attention to the disjunction or conflict of laws (Dodson, 1995; Gaykamangu, 2012). Bowen (2021a: 21–2) points out that 'Aboriginal law (or aspects of it) can be invisible or dismissed by settler Australians as merely culture or "lore"'.

Land claims and native title hearings are the site of arguably the most extreme cases of mismatch in cultural presuppositions, as explored in the work of anthropological linguists, including Frances Morphy (2007) and Walsh (1995, 2008). At the basis of this mismatch are fundamental cultural and epistemological differences in understandings about the social, physical and spiritual world. Central Anglo-legal concepts such as land ownership and permission have no equivalents in the traditional Aboriginal societies and languages.

Further, while the Anglo-Australian legal system 'is founded on the principle that the maximum possible amount of information should be available publicly and freely' (Gray, 2000: 189), in Aboriginal societies there is typically a range of restrictions on sharing, knowledge, particularly traditional knowledge. However, traditional knowledge is highly valued in the formal legal assessment of claims about connection to land. Other disjunctions arise in terms of what counts as proof, for example of historical connection. Here the frequent Aboriginal reliance on performance of ceremony, song and art often contrasts with the formal legal tradition priority given to written documents, forming part of the 'inevitable clash between Indigenous and non-indigenous modes of proof' about land ownership (ibid.: 186).

Fundamental cultural differences between the formal legal system and Aboriginal law also arise in the assumed universality of the western concept of individual rights. Thus, the right to silence in a police interview relies on assumptions, such as 'individuals can choose autonomously how to behave, unless they are constrained by law' (Bowen, 2019: 8). Bowen argues that some Aboriginal people 'may not share these assumptions because they live in societies with a different balance between personal-internal agency and other compelling forces inherent in a person's place in society'. Bowen's work (2019, 2021a, 2021b) shows that the caution (= right to silence) text 'is not suitable for diverse audiences' and he argues that 'those unfamiliar with its underlying culture will struggle to understand it'.

The central role of legal culture itself for second language speakers is also explored in relation to interpreting and translation, by Cooke (e.g. 1995b) and Bowen (2021b), who both highlight problems with the notion of translation without explanation, which is referred to as direct translation. Cooke (1995b) discusses an example from the translation of the findings of a 1990/1991 coronial inquest into the death of an Aboriginal person from an Arnhem Land community where little English was spoken. He shows that it is impossible for an interpreter or translator to make some texts meaningful when they are professionally 'precluded from providing explication and explanation as an integral process of translation across divergent cultures' (p. 37).

Bowen's work on the language of the police caution also highlights the limitations of a purely linguistic approach to explaining legal language to many Aboriginal people. He argues (2021a) that telling a suspect that a police interview can be 'used in evidence' (a typical expression used in the communication of the right to silence) is only meaningful if the suspect not only knows the word 'evidence' but also has prior contextual knowledge about how evidence is used in criminal trials, that is, knowledge about the culture of the law.

Bowen (2021b) further discusses some problems in the translation of the right to silence caution in police interviews for suspects for whom a direct translation is unable to capture important implicatures in meaning. He points out that many non-native speakers might not understand that the police saying, 'you don't have to say anything' implies a legal right. This includes the implication that neither police, during the interview or later, nor the judge or jury, when the case goes to court, can take any actions or draw any conclusions about the suspect's guilt based on them choosing not to say anything in the interview. In contrast, he shows that the translated cautions in two of the most commonly spoken languages in the Northern Territory (Djambarrpuyngu and Kriol, see Section 3.6.2) make this information explicit. This results in an indirect translation, which Bowen (2021b: 317) explains as

> aiming to communicate the caution by working with context actually available to the target audience [ie Djambarrpuyngu and Kriol speakers], which means explicitly supplying further context which [is] available to the source audience [ie native speakers of English, or maybe those who are legally informed, see Bowen 2021b: 320], but not the target audience.

This 'explicitation' approach is not universally accepted within the field of translation studies, as it could be seen to breach the ethical code which states that 'translators do not alter, add to, or omit anything from the content and intent of the source message' (AUSIT, 2012:10, cited in Bowen, 2021b: 319).

5.2 Socioculturally Specific Challenges Impacting Interaction

At the interactional level, translation and interpreting are essential to legal processes with people and communities in remote Australia. However, translation and interpreting can also be very difficult, or even impossible, where the topics being discussed are outside the sociocultural experience of one of the parties (Cooke 1995b; Morphy, 2007; Bowen, 2021a). Thus, as Morphy illustrates, normally routine courtroom proceedings, such as asking a witness to recognise a typed (English) version of their earlier oral statement (in their home language) to their lawyer, can become complex and fraught. In her analysis of a Native Title Federal Court hearing in Arnhem Land, Morphy describes the witness statement as 'an instance of "enforced commensurability" in the context of an unequal power relation' (2007: 40). This fundamental challenge to even the most apparently routine communication practices in court is not limited to land claims and native title (see Cooke, 1995b: 71–2).

Sociocultural context can also cause challenges in communities with small numbers of speakers (such as in remote Australia) for the essential interpreter requirement of impartiality. In his research in Western Australia, Cooke (2004) discusses these challenges and ways in which Aboriginal interpreting services address this issue (see also Rusho, 2021).

Eades' research (e.g. 2013) with Aboriginal speakers of varieties of English has also highlighted pragmatic issues arising from the central role of interviews in legal processes, including lawyer-client interviews, police interviews or in courtroom hearings. The legal reliance on interviews contrasts with the ways in which people seek extensive, sensitive or complex information in Aboriginal societies. This occurs typically in a much less direct way, in which reciprocal talk and relationships are crucial, and take precedence over concerns with time and efficiency in finding out information. Many difficulties can arise in legal settings which involve Aboriginal people who do not have strong bicultural abilities in communication, and in which (non-Aboriginal) legal practitioners are often unaware of the impact of these sociocultural differences.

One of these difficulties concerns the interpretation of arguably one of the simplest English words, 'yes' (Section 2.3.5). Eades (2013) explains cultural factors involved in the widespread Aboriginal use of minimal answers of apparent agreement, such as 'yes', in answer to direct questions, for social reasons such as cooperating with 'whitefella questions'. Anthropologists and judges have observed this pattern, now referred to as 'gratuitous concurrence', for over a century (see Eades, 2013; Mildren, 1999, Gray 2022/2023). However, it can be difficult for some lawyers, judges and police officers to recognise this challenge to the referential language ideology (Sections 2.3.5 and 3.6.1).

For more than three decades, Eades has responded to lawyers' requests for expert reports relating to conversational style and the relevance of sociocultural context in communication with Aboriginal people. In some of these cases she has also presented oral evidence. The following list provides summary information about the lawyers' questions addressed in some of these cases:

- lawyers' inability to take instructions from their client about circumstances of her offence, despite her being able to explain her story to her counsellor at the same time, and a few years later to a culturally sensitive TV journalist; appeal against murder conviction, *R v Kina* 1993 (Eades, 2003)
- issues that should be explained by the court to the jury about specific features of Aboriginal use of English that might be relevant to the evidence of fifty Aboriginal witnesses from a northern NSW community; Supreme Court murder trial, *R v Hart* 2006 (Eades, 2016a)

- cultural appropriateness of government department's information-seeking processes with a NSW Aboriginal woman; appeal against administrative decision relating to family status, *Lynwood v Secretary, Department of Education, Employment and Workplace Relations and Anor* 2011
- the extent to which police questioning of witnesses to the detention of a man who died in a police cell exemplified good communication with Aboriginal witnesses (one of many issues examined in this case); *Wootton & Ors v Queensland & Anor* 2016, aka 'Palm Island Racial Discrimination Case', Australia's largest racial discrimination case
- specific features of Aboriginal use of English that might be relevant to the evidence of a large number of Aboriginal witnesses from Queensland. *Pearson v Queensland* 2020, aka 'Queensland Stolen Wages Case', Australia's largest human rights case
- communication and linguistic issues involved in the draft of the notice to be sent to group members (people held in youth detention between 2011 and 2017) in a successful class action, *Jenkings v Northern Territory of Australia* (No 4) 2021, aka 'Northern Territory Youth Justice Class Action'
- whether it was more likely than not that nine specific Aboriginal consumers had used gratuitous concurrence in fifty of their phone calls with insurance salespeople; *ASIC v Select AFSL* 2022. (This detailed and lengthy report was prepared with considerable assistance from Alex Bowen.) This is the first judicial decision in the civil jurisdiction to accept linguistic evidence about gratuitous concurrence (Gray, 2022/23).

5.3 Other Socioculturally Specific Assumptions

In addition to the socioculturally specific assumptions about communication and interaction, there may be other types of socioculturally specific assumptions presupposed in lawyer questions which are not shared with the Aboriginal witness. And, conversely, there may be socioculturally specific assumptions presupposed in witness answers which are not shared with the lawyer. A telling example comes from Cooke's (1995a) work with Aboriginal witnesses in a coronial inquiry in a remote area of Arnhem Land in the Northern Territory. Cooke explains a particular miscommunication between a lawyer and a witness to a fatal attack by police on a mentally ill man. At the heart of the miscommunication was the contrast between the Anglo view which separates mental and physical health (distinguishing the 'sickness in his head' from 'anything wrong with his body or wrong with him physically'), and the Aboriginal view that sees the two as inseparable (as the witness puts it, the man had something wrong 'from his head to his body'). The cross-examination of the witness reveals the cultural presupposition in the lawyer's questioning that although the deceased may have suffered from a mental illness, he had nothing 'wrong with his body', as evidenced by the fact that he 'could walk long' distances. The Aboriginal witness, on the other hand, interpreted the deceased's tendency to go for long walks on his own, as a symptom of 'his sickness', which pervaded his whole being 'from his head to his body'.

But it is not only in remote traditionally oriented Aboriginal communities that sociocultural context has been found to impact understanding and communication in the law. Eades' (2000) courtroom study in a NSW town (Section 4.2.2) found that cultural presuppositions about social life played an important part in several instances in which Aboriginal witnesses were prevented from telling their story by their own lawyer, and in some cases by the judge. This silencing of witnesses was brought about sometimes by the lawyer or judge interrupting the witness, and at other times by metalinguistic comments about how to answer a particular question, such as 'I don't think it's an answer to the question'. It appeared to occur particularly in situations where legal professionals (whether lawyer or judge) were ignorant about fundamental aspects of the everyday cultural values and practices of Aboriginal people, such as family structure and obligations, and residential arrangements.

Perhaps it is not surprising that most of the forensic linguistic work involving sociocultural context has highlighted issues impacting the participation of Aboriginal people in the law. The overrepresentation of Aboriginal people in the criminal justice process has been a major concern for the law, as well as criminology and some linguists for more than three decades now (Eades, 2012). Further, the differences in culture and societies between Aboriginal Australia and the culture of the law can be remarkable, as some of the examples indicate. But there is no reason to think that the law's lack of awareness about sociocultural contexts is relevant only to Aboriginal people, especially given the rich linguistic and cultural diversity in Australia.

Muniroh, Findling and Heydon (2018) point out that concern about the culturally specific nature of investigative interviewing is also relevant to the tribunal which hears appeals from asylum seekers whose applications have been rejected by immigration officials in the refugee status determination process. They suggest that the interviewing framework of the tribunal could be enriched by incorporating some strategies from the cognitive interviewing approach to police interviews (see Section 4.1.1).

Smith-Khan's (2017) focus on institutional texts, rather than interviews, in the refugee status determination process shows that guidance-writers and decision-makers are aware of cultural difference as a complicating factor when assessing asylum applications. But in the process of deciding how much to believe of what applicants say, tribunal decision-makers have been shown to essentialise the culture of applicants. This has resulted in expectations that asylum seekers should act in stereotypical ways consistent with generalisations about their particular sociocultural group. At the same time, decision makers problematically position themselves as neutral and having no culture, and thus capable of objectivity, consistent with their institutional guidance (see also Section 4.2.4).

6 Engagement, Expansion and Expectation

6.1 Introduction

This Element has chronicled the development of forensic linguistics in Australia and outlined contributions made by individuals and networks of scholars across a range of specialisations and applications in the field. In this final section we highlight some characteristics of forensic linguistics in Australia, while not claiming that these features are unique to our country. A recurrent theme has been the role that Australian linguists have played in responding to misconceptions and problematic language ideologies that can undermine just processes in the law.

We begin this section by recognising the important role of some members of the judiciary and the legal profession in addressing language issues, especially in relation to just processes in the law (Section 6.2). This is followed by an outline of the law's recognition of specific Australian forensic linguistic work (Section 6.3). The Appendix gives specific details that provide evidence of the law's engagement with, and recognition of, forensic linguistics. While there has been less engagement by law enforcement, Section 6.4 outlines some examples. Sections 6.5 and 6.6 overview the interdisciplinary and international engagement of forensic linguists.

We conclude this Element in Section 6.7 with our characterisation of much of the forensic linguistic work in Australia as critical forensic linguistics, highlighting some of the key factors that motivate and support this approach.

6.2 Engagement of the Judiciary and Legal Profession with Forensic Linguistics

Consideration of the law's engagement with forensic linguistics must start by recognising that within the Australian judiciary and legal profession there has been some awareness of the close connection between language and fairness in the law since before this was a topic considered by linguists. This is particularly the situation in the Northern Territory, where Aboriginal people currently make up 26 per cent of the population, but 83 per cent of the prison population (the highest rate in Australia on both measures).

Attention must be drawn to (the late) Justice Sir William Forster of the Northern Territory Supreme Court 1971–1985, whose seminal 1976 judgment in *R v Anunga* carefully set out and explained nine guidelines for police interrogation of Aboriginal people. Beginning with the circumstances in which an interpreter is required, three of the guidelines directly address language issues.

The third guideline stipulates that the right to silence 'should be explained in simple terms and the suspect should be asked to state, phrase by phrase, what it means'. This predated by four decades the work of the international Communication of Rights Group (Section 3.5.2), in its formulation of guidelines for communicating rights to non-native speakers (cf CoRG 2015 'Adopt an in-your-own-words requirement').

Justice Forster's observation that 'most Aboriginal people ... will answer questions by white people in the way they think the questioner wants' foreshadowed linguistic work about gratuitous concurrence (Section 5.2), and followed judicial recognition of the problems caused by this communicative practice, which had been raised in 1960 by Justice Kriewaldt from the same jurisdiction (see *Anunga* paragraph 3; 4th Guideline; Eades, 2008a: 92–3). Widely referred to as the Anunga Rules, these guidelines form the basis of similar guidelines in other Australian jurisdictions, and are regularly cited in courts and judicial decisions throughout the country.

Judicial leadership on language and law in the Northern Territory has continued, particularly with Justice Dean Mildren (now retired), and with the Supreme Court in that jurisdiction organising conferences on language and the law involving participation beyond the judiciary (not customary for Australian courts). Both Justice Mildren's initiatives and the Supreme Court conferences have involved engagement with forensic linguists, as indicated in the Appendix.

The Judicial Committee on Cultural Diversity has played a prominent role in two major language and the law initiatives. In addition to the development of the *National Standards* for interpreters (Section 2.3.3), this national judicial organisation received the Linguistics Call to Action to which its Chair, Chris Kourakis (Chief Justice of South Australia) responded constructively by holding a consultation in which he and three other judges (Justice Helen Bowskill, Supreme Court of Queensland; Chief Judge Kevin Sleight, District Court of Western Australia; Justice Helen Wood, Supreme Court of Tasmania) heard the linguists' views (Section 3.1.3).

While key judges have provided judicial leadership on language issues, and engaged with forensic linguistics, a small number of linguists and lawyer-linguists have also led the way in informing lawyers about language issues, as well as in working on plain English versions of legal terminology and of the police caution to speakers of Aboriginal languages (Section 3.5.2).

Since the early 1990s, Australian forensic linguists have been actively involved in providing professional workshops and training for lawyers, law students, judicial officers and, to a lesser extent, law enforcement officers: e.g. Alex Bowen, Michael Cooke, Diana Eades, Helen Fraser, Ben Grimes, Georgina Heydon and Sandra Hale.

But, for many forensic linguists, not only in Australia, the richest engagement with the judiciary is with Federal Court Judge Peter Gray (now retired), who has been directly and actively involved for two decades, as detailed in the Appendix.

6.3 Recognition in Law of Specific Australian Forensic Linguistics Work

6.3.1 In Legal Proceedings

Beginning with the Queensland criminal case of *R v Aubrey* 1995, the work of Diana Eades on communicating with Aboriginal people in the law has been cited in several cases where no expert linguistic evidence has been provided (see Appendix). In another such case, *R v BL* 2015, in addition to citing Eades' work, the judicial decision also cites the work of Michael Cooke, and the *Guidelines for Communicating Rights to Non-Native Speakers of English in Australia, England and Wales, and the USA* (CoRG, 2015, Section 3.5.2).

The most important case to cite linguistic research is *Nguyen v R* 2020 in which the High Court of Australia (our highest court) decided an issue involving fairness in the prosecution of people 'with cultural and linguistic disadvantage' (with no specific reference to Aboriginal people). Justice Edelman's judgment includes the adoption of Eades' work about the difficulties involved in giving an account of events (or telling and retelling your story, Section 4.2.3) within the constraints of police interview and courtroom questioning, referring to Eades (2012). This judgment marks a new development in the awareness by lawyers and judges of linguistic research, particularly because there was no expert linguistic evidence in this case. It also marks a step forward in our legal system's understanding and recognition of the consequences of linguistic and cultural diversity.

6.3.2 In Commissioned Reports, Judicial Benchbooks and Similar

Michael Cooke, Sandra Hale and Georgina Heydon have all produced reports commissioned by legal organisations, as indicated in the Appendix. The Appendix also provides evidence of reports and other publications produced for judicial officers by researchers and support staff of courts and tribunals that have drawn on the work of Michael Cooke, Diana Eades and Sandra Hale, for more than two decades.

6.4 Engagement of Law Enforcement with Forensic Linguistics

Compared to the judiciary and legal profession, law enforcement has had a more limited engagement with forensic linguistics.

Georgina Heydon has contributed to sociolinguistic, cross-cultural communication and interviewing training for law enforcement officers in South Australia Police Service, the Australian Federal Police and Queensland Police Service. She has also worked in partnership with Victoria and NSW Police Services on research into child interviewing and informal reporting of sexual assault.

Lawyer-linguist Ben Grimes worked closely with police in the Northern Territory as part of the multi-party group which developed the recorded police cautions in Aboriginal languages. This group included the Aboriginal Interpreter Service. And in Western Australia, lawyer-linguist Alex Bowen contributed to a similar project with police and Aboriginal Interpreting Western Australia (Section 3.5.2).

Diana Eades participated in a lengthy recorded interview used in training material commissioned by NSW Police about communicating with Aboriginal people. This resulted from one of the recommendations of the New South Wales Parliament Standing Committee on Law and Justice Inquiry (2014), which investigated the many ways in which the state's legal system had failed the families of three murdered Aboriginal children over more than two decades.

Over many years Sandra Hale has engaged in professional dialogue with the NSW Police Diversity Trainer Judy Saba.

6.5 Interdisciplinary Engagement of Forensic Linguists

As the reference list attests, Australian forensic linguists are increasingly publishing in a wide range of legal journals and newsletters. Of particular note is the 2021 special issue (30, 4) of *Griffith Law Review* 2021 on 'Linguistic diversity as a challenge for legal policy', edited by Alexandra Grey and Laura Smith-Khan, which features articles by several Australian linguists and lawyers.

Collaborations with psychologists are found in the work of Sandra Hale (e.g. Hale et al., 2017, 2019, 2020, 2022), Helen Fraser (e.g. Fraser & Stevenson, 2014) and Georgina Heydon (e.g. La Rooy et al., 2015).

In an example of a collaboration not often represented in the international forensic linguistic literature, linguists Georgina Heydon, Dian Muniroh, Ceyhan Kurt and Andy Roh collaborate with critical criminologists in publications that address sexual assault reporting, racial discrimination and other ideologies underlying justice processes expressed through language policies (Heydon & Powell, 2018; Muniroh et al., 2018; MacFarlane et al., 2019; Loney-Howes, Heydon & O'Neill, 2021).

6.6 International Engagement of Forensic Linguists

Australian linguists have been prominent in the development of two sets of international guidelines intended to communicate the findings of linguistic research and experience to relevant professionals: about language analysis in refugee cases (Section 3.3), and communicating rights to non-native speakers of English (Section 3.5.2).

While a number of linguists in the UK and the USA are continuing to contribute to police investigative interviewing research and practice, Australian linguists, including Heydon, were early to adapt their findings to a practice environment. Their work has also inspired linguistic engagement with police training in other countries, such as Mozambique (Mabasso, 2019), South Africa (Ralarala, 2016) and Indonesia (Muniroh & Heydon, 2022). Although the published work does not always reflect the practical application of Australian linguistic research to police interviewing training, the personal experiences of the authors and those in their network confirm that a few Australians are very active in this regard. Heydon, for instance, has delivered training on linguistic structures that underpin good practice interviewing (see Heydon, 2012, Heydon & Mabasso, 2018) to police academies and judicial colleges in Australia, South Africa, Mozambique, Pakistan, the Philippines, Indonesia, China, Canada, the USA, Sweden, the European Police College, Belgium and France.

6.7 Conclusion

The work of forensic linguists in providing expert evidence requires focused attention on specific questions, and (typically) specific data. But, when it comes to research and its practical applications, in many ways we could characterise the field in Australia as critical forensic linguistics, that is, forensic linguistics that engages with questions of power and inequality. This is driven by many factors, including:

- the recognition that language issues are often involved in failures of the justice system, and that misconceptions and problematic ideologies about language in the law can have consequences not only for individual participants in particular legal processes, but can contribute more widely to social inequalities,
- the strong awareness in Australian linguistics of the linguistic and cultural richness of the many Indigenous societies, combined with the shocking overrepresentation of Aboriginal people in the criminal justice process and in prisons throughout the country,
- the increasing multilingualism of Australia, combined with the impact of both the growing field of interpreting and translation studies and the two

professional organisations: Australian Institute of Interpreters and Translators (AUSIT) and the national standards and certifying authority for translators and interpreters in Australia (NAATI). Sandra Hale has served a term as President of the former, and Michael Cooke has served a term as a Director of the latter,

- the recognition of the importance of the wider legal, social and cultural contexts in which forensic linguistic research and practical applications take place,
- the knowledge that we live in a country where scholars can have opportunities to present the findings of our research beyond the academy to people who want to listen. In this way we can sometimes be part of change in the justice system,
- experiences of productive and meaningful discussions with judicial officers, lawyers and, to a lesser extent, law enforcement officers, about language issues.

Reflecting on the last three decades of Australian forensic linguists, we would like to express respect and appreciation for those before us who broke new ground in applying linguistics to the law. We have been privileged to be part of the journey of forging the new subdiscipline of forensic linguistics, and engaging in transdisciplinary exchange about language and law, especially with practitioners and other experts in the law. This broader and deeper engagement of linguists in the law is now greatly enriched by increasing numbers of lawyers and others with legal training who are embracing linguistics in further study and research. We confidently expect that our field will intensify its impact within both linguistics and the law.

List of Abbreviations

AAAL	Applied Linguistics Association of Australia
AIJA	Austral(as)ian Institute of Judicial Administration
AIWA	Aboriginal Interpreting Western Australia
ARC	Australian Research Council
ASSTA	Austral(as)ian Speech Science and Technology Association
AUSIT	Australian Institute of Interpreters and Translators
CCJ	Council of Chief Justices
FSSSC	Forensic Speech Science Standards Committee (Re-formed in 2004 as Forensic Speech Science Committee, FSSC)
IAFL	International Association of Forensic Linguists (Name changed in 2021 to IAFLL
IAFLL	International Association for Forensic and Legal Linguistics (before 2021: IAFL)
IAFP	International Association for Forensic Phonetics (now: IAFPA)
IAFPA	International Association for Forensic Phonetics and Acoustics (formerly: IAFP)
JCCD	Judicial Council on Cultural Diversity
LAAP	Language Analysis in the Asylum Process
LADO	Language Analysis for the Determination of Origin
LLIRN	Law and Linguistics Interdisciplinary Researchers' Network
LR	Likelihood Ratio
National Standards	Recommended National Standards for Working with Interpreters in Courts and Tribunals National Standards
SCAN	Scientific Content Analysis

Appendix

Engagement of the Judiciary and Legal Profession with Forensic Linguistics

(Retired) Justice Dean Mildren, Northern Territory Supreme Court, 1991–2013

- leading Australian judicial officer on language and communication issues impacting participation of Aboriginal people in the law
- combines his extensive experience with attention to linguistic research, and his discussions and collaboration with linguist Michael Cooke, in publications (e.g. Mildren, 1999), keynote conference addresses (e.g. Mildren, 2012) and judgments (e.g. *R v Kenny Charlie* 1995),
- has long recognised the role of gratuitous concurrence (see Section 5.2) in rendering some Aboriginal people too suggestible for the fair use of leading questions in cross-examination; highlights the relevance of the trial judge's power 'to disallow questions, or forms of questions, which are unfair' (e.g. Mildren, 1997: 14, also CJC, 1996: 52).
- in early 1990s pioneered directions to juries about Aboriginal ways of using English; versions in CJC (1996): A9–11 prepared in collaboration with Diana Eades, and for Torres Strait Islanders with Helen Harper (see also Mildren, 1997, 1999). Also published in Queensland Supreme Court's 2016 *Equal Treatment Benchbook* (Chapter 9: Appendix B) and discussed in equivalent WA and NSW publications (Fryer-Smith, 2008; Judicial Commission of New South Wales, 2022). See Eades (2016a) for discussion.
- also played a central role in the development of the *National Standards* for interpreters in courts and tribunals (see Section 3.6.2), working extensively with linguist Sandra Hale on drafting this document.

The Northern Territory Supreme Court

- has organised three interdisciplinary language and law conferences (2012, 2015, 2019), bringing together interpreters representing numerous languages (Aboriginal and immigrant) spoken in the Territory, with judges, lawyers, linguists and a few police officers.
- two linguists actively involved from the beginning of the planning: linguist-interpreter David Moore and lawyer-linguist Ben Grimes

- organisation and major focus on Northern Territory languages and law, but participants also from several other jurisdictions
- combination of various presentation formats, enabling many people to speak
- 'reverse role plays', prepared and presented by interpreters in conjunction with lawyers, show some common experiences of professional interpreters in legal settings. (See www.ictv.com.au/video/item/2477. Justice Mildren – see above – acting as an accused person appearing in an Aboriginal court, where no-one speaks his language, charged with breaking Aboriginal laws.)

Federal Court Justice Peter Gray (now retired)

- twenty-nine years as Federal Court Judge included several years as Aboriginal Land Commissioner
- active member of IAFLL since 2003; member of the Executive Committee for two four-year terms
- legal expertise and experience, strong interest in language and linguistics, and active support of scholars and students have been much valued in the Australian and international forensic linguistics communities for over two decades
- published in the field (e.g. 2011, 2021, 2022/23)
- gained Masters of Applied Linguistics (University of New England, 2019)
- has developed, with John Gibbons, the only language and law course in an Australian university Law School; taught by them and colleagues in 2015, 2018, 2020 and 2022; at Monash University Law School, where Gray is a Distinguished Affiliate and Teaching Associate.

Recognition in Law of Specific Australian Forensic Linguistics Work

In Legal Proceedings

In addition to the cases in Section 6.3.1: Queensland (*R v D* 2003), the Northern Territory (*Dumoo v Garner* 1998) and Western Australia (*Stack v WA* 2004).

In an unreported 2017 case in the Magistrate's Court in a remote Western Australian city, a magistrate requested that a defence lawyer for an Aboriginal defendant 'contact Diana Eades for a report on the communication between police and the accused' in his police interview;

during a period of state-wide discussion of the judgment in the *Gibson* case (see Section 3.5.1) about failings in police interviews of Aboriginal partial speakers of English. Eades' report was accepted by the magistrate who subsequently ruled the police interview in this case as legally inadmissible.

In Commissioned Reports, Judicial Benchbooks and Similar

by *Australian (now Australasian) Institute of Judicial Administration* (AIJA):

  i) Cooke (2002) on Indigenous interpreting issues for courts
 ii) Hale's (2011) national survey of interpreter policies, practices and proto-cols in Australian courts and tribunals, which resulted from the highly successful 2009 AIJA national conference on interpreters in courts and tribunals. A key role played by Professor Greg Reinhardt, Executive Director of AIJA from 1997 to 2020.

    This report and a recommendation of the conference directly led to the drafting, consultation and publication of the ground-breaking *National Standards* for working with interpreters in courts and tribu-nals (first edition 2017, second edition 2022, see Sections 2.3.3, 3.6.2 and 6.2).

iii) Greg Reinhardt has also taken an active interest in forensic linguistics more broadly (see Section 3.1.3) and attended several international IAFL conferences over a number of years, as well as providing encour-agement and support to forensic linguists to publish in AIJA's journal, *Journal of Judicial Administration)* (Cooke, 2009; Findling & Heydon, 2016; Eades, 2018; Fraser, 2018). See also Section 3.1.3 for his involvement in bringing the linguists' Call to Action to judicial attention.

 iv) *by (then) Refugee Review Tribunal and Migration Review Tribunal*: report and training programme from Heydon that provided guidelines for the questioning of applicants using cognitive interviewing methods; reported in Findling and Heydon (2016).

  v) *by (Melbourne) South East Centre Against Sexual Assault:* unpublished report describing the elicitation of sexual assault narratives in informal, online settings by Heydon and criminologist Rachel Loney-Howes (Loney-Howes & Heydon, 2018; see also Loney-Howes et al., 2021 for more extensive findings from follow-up research).

vi) *by Criminal Justice Commission Queensland* (1996): about Aboriginal witnesses in court: research of Cooke and Eades

vii) *by Judicial Commission of NSW* (2022): research of Eades and Hale

viii) *by Queensland Supreme Court* (2016) *and Fryer-Smith (2008):* research of Eades

Cases Cited

* indicates expert linguistic evidence or linguistic research discussed or referred to in judgment

* *(ASIC) Australian Securities and Investments Commission v Select AFSL Pty Ltd* (No 2) [2022] FCA 786

* *Australian Prudential Regulation Authority v Siminton* (No 7) [2007] FCA 1609 (7 November 2007)

Butera v DPP (VIC) [1987] HCA 58

Crawford v Venardos & Ors [1995] Brisbane Magistrates' Court, Unreported, 24 February

* *Dumoo v Garner* [1998] NTSC 8; 7 NTLR 129

* *Jenkings v Northern Territory of Australia* (No 4) [2021] FCA 839

* *JBS Australia Pty Ltd v Australian Meat Group Pty Ltd* [2017] FCA 1421

* *Lynwood and Secretary, Department of Education, Employment and Workplace Relations and Anor* [2011] AATA 213

* *Mason v R* (No. 1) [2015] NSWCCA 324

* *Medical Board of Australia v Roberts* [2014] Western Australian State Administrative Tribunal 76.

* *Nguyen v R* [2020] HCA 23

* *N.V. Sumatra Tobacco Trading Company v British American Tobacco Services Limited* [2011] FCA 1051

Pearson v Queensland [2020] No 2, FCA 619

R v Anunga, R v Wheeler [1976] NTSC 11 ALR 412

* *R v Aubrey* [1995] Unreported, Queensland Court of Appeal, 28 April.

* *R v BL* [2015] NTSC 85

* *R v Condren* [1987] Queensland Court of Criminal Appeal *Australian Criminal Reports* 28, 261–299.

* *R v D* [2003] QCA 347, 139 A Crim R 509

* *R v Gilmore* [1977] 2 NSWLR 9351977

R v Hart [2006] NSWSC 1501, Unreported, 7 July.

* *R v Izumi* [1995] QSC Unreported, 22 May.

R v Kenny Charlie [1995] NTSC Unreported, 28 September.

R v Kina [1993] QCA, Unreported, 29 November.

R v M [1995] WASC, Unreported, February.

* *R v McHardie and Danielson* [1983] 2 NSWLR 733

References

Aboriginal Resource and Development Services (ARDS). (2008). *An Absence of Mutual Respect: Bäyŋu Ḏayaŋu-Ḏapmaranhamirr Rom ga Ḏorra*. https://ards.com.au/resources/downloadable/an-absence-of-mutual-respect-b%C3%A4y%C5%8Bu-%C5%8Baya%C5%8Bu-%E1%B8%8Fapmaranhamirr-rom-ga-%C5%8Borra/.

———. (2015). *Dhuwal Wäyukpuy: Rom Dhäruk Mala ga Mayali'* [Legal Dictionary Djambarrpuyngu]. www.ards.com.au/resources-2/p/legal-dictionary-djambarrpuyngu.

Aboriginal Resource and Development Services (ARDS), North Australian Aboriginal Justice Agency (NAAJA), & Aboriginal Interpreter Service, Northern Territory Government (AIS). (2015). *The Plain English Legal Dictionary: Northern Territory Criminal Law. A Resource for Judicial Officers, Aboriginal Interpreters and Legal Professionals Working with Speakers of Aboriginal Languages*. https://ards.com.au/uploads/Downloads/15/39-15.Legal_Dictionary_plain_English_version.pdf.

Adam, L., & van Golde, C. (2020). Police practice and false confessions: A search for the implementation of investigative interviewing in Australia. *Alternative Law Journal*, 45(1), 52–9.

Alderman, T. (2005). *Forensic Speaker Identification: A Likelihood Ratio-based Approach Using Vowel Formants*. Munich: Lincom GmBH.

AUSIT (Australian Institute of Interpreters and Translators). (2012). *AUSIT Code of Ethics and Code of Conduct*. https://ausit.org/wp-content/uploads/2020/02/Code_Of_Ethics_Full.pdf.

Baldwin, J. R., & French, P. (1990). *Forensic Phonetics*. London: Pinter.

Blommaert, J. (2005). *Discourse: A Critical Introduction*. Cambridge: Cambridge University Press.

Bowden, P., Henning, T., & Plater, D. (2014). Balancing fairness to victims, society and defendants in the cross-examination of vulnerable witnesses: An impossible triangulation? *Melbourne University Law Review*, 37, 539–84.

Bowe, H., & Storey, K. (1995). Linguistic analysis as evidence of speaker identification: Demand and response. In Eades, ed., pp. 187–200.

Bowen, A. (2019). 'You don't have to say anything': Modality and consequences in conversations about the right to silence in the Northern Territory. *Australian Journal of Linguistics*, 39(3), 347–74.

———. (2021a). Explaining the right to silence under Anunga: 40 years of a policy about language. *Griffith Law Review*, 30(1), 18–49.

(2021b). Intercultural translation of vague legal language: The right to silence in the Northern Territory of Australia. *Target: International Journal of Translation Studies*, 33(2), 308–40.

(2021c). Supporting two-way communication with police in Western Australia: New translation app helps to identify need for Aboriginal interpreters. *Brandeis University. Language, Culture and Justice Hub. Spotlight.* www.brandeis.edu/ethics/international-justice/language-culture-justice/spotlight-oct-2021.html.

Bowen, A., & Eades, D. (2022). Forensic linguistics and pseudoscience: How to recognise the difference. *Precedent*, 172, 35–9.

Brennan, G. (1979). *The Need for Interpreting and Translation Services for Australian Aboriginals, with Special Reference to the Northern Territory: A Research Report*. Canberra: Department of Aboriginal Affairs.

Brennan, M. (1995). The discourse of denial: Cross-examining child victim witnesses. *Journal of Pragmatics*, 23, 71–91.

Brennan, M., & Brennan, R. (1988). *Strange Language: Child Victims under Cross-Examination*, 2nd ed. Wagga Wagga: Charles Sturt University.

Candlin, C., & Maley, Y. (1997). Intertextuality and interdiscursivity in the discourse of alternative dispute resolution. In B.-L. Gunnarson, P. Linell & B. Nordberg, eds., *The Construction of Professional Discourse*. London: Longman, pp. 200–22.

Chan, R. (2020). The empirical psychological science behind ad hoc expert voice identification evidence. *University of Tasmania Law Review*, 39(1), 23–38.

Communication of Rights Group (CoRG). (2015). *Guidelines for Communication of Rights to Non-native Speakers of English*. www.aaal.org/guidelines-for-communication-rights.

Conley, J. M., O'Barr, W. M., & Conley Riner, R. (2019). *Just Words: Law, Language, and Power*, 3rd ed. London: University of Chicago Press.

Cooke, M. (1995a). Aboriginal evidence in the cross-cultural courtroom. In Eades, ed., pp. 55–96.

(1995b). Understood by all concerned? Anglo/Aboriginal legal translation. In M. Morris, ed., *Translation and the Law*. Amsterdam: John Benjamins, pp. 37–66.

(1996). A different story: Narrative versus 'question and answer' in Aboriginal evidence. *Forensic Linguistics*, 3(2), 273–88.

(2002). *Indigenous Interpreting Issues for the Courts*. Carlton: Australian Institute of Judicial Administration.

(2004). *Caught in the Middle: Indigenous Interpreters and Customary Law*. Background Paper No. 2. Law Reform Commission of Western Australia. www.lrc.justice.wa.gov.au/.

(2009). Anglo/Aboriginal communication in the criminal justice process: A collective responsibility. *Journal of Judicial Administration*, 19(1), 26–35.

Coulthard, M., May, A., & Sousa-Silva, R. (eds.). (2020). *The Routledge Handbook of Forensic Linguistics*, 2nd ed. London: Routledge.

Criminal Justice Commission (CJC). (1996). *Aboriginal Witnesses in Queensland's Criminal Courts*. Brisbane: Criminal Justice Commission.

Deamer, F., Fraser, H., Haworth, K. et al. (eds.). (2022). *Capturing Talk: The Institutional Practices Surrounding the Transcription of Spoken Language*. Frontiers in Communication. www.frontiersin.org/research-topics/19744/capturing-talk-the-institutional-practices-surrounding-the-transcription-of-spoken-language.

Dieckmann, C., & Rojas-Lizana, I. (2016). The pragmatics of legal advice services in a community legal centre in Australia: Domination or facilitation? *International Journal of Speech Language and the Law*, 23 (2), 167–93.

Dodson, M. (1995). From 'lore' to 'law': Indigenous rights and Australian legal systems. *Aboriginal Law Bulletin*, 72(3), 1–3.

Eades, D. (1992). *Aboriginal English and the Law: Communicating with Aboriginal English Speaking Clients: A Handbook for Legal Practitioners*. Brisbane: Queensland Law Society.

(1993). The case for Condren: Aboriginal English, pragmatics and the law. *Journal of Pragmatics*, 20(2), 141–62.

(1994). Forensic linguistics in Australia: An overview. *International Journal of Speech Language and the Law*, 1(2), 113–32.

(ed.). (1995). *Language in Evidence: Issues Confronting Aboriginal and Multicultural Australia*. Sydney: University of New South Wales Press.

(2000). 'I don't think it's an answer to the question': Silencing Aboriginal witnesses in court. *Language in Society*, 29(2), 161–96.

(2003). 'I don't think the lawyers were communicating with me': Misunderstanding cultural differences in communicative style. *Emory Law Journal*, 52, 1109–34.

(2005). Applied linguistics and language analysis in asylum seeker cases. *Applied Linguistics*, 26(4), 503–26.

(2008a). *Courtroom Talk and Neocolonial Control*. Berlin: Mouton de Gruyter.

(2008b). Telling and retelling your story in court: Questions, assumptions and intercultural implications. *Current Issues in Criminal Justice*, 20(2), 209–30.

(2009). Testing the claims of asylum seekers: The role of language analysis. *Language Assessment Quarterly*, 6(1), 30–40.

(2010). *Sociolinguistics and the Legal Process*. Bristol: Multilingual Matters.

(2012). The social consequences of language ideologies in courtroom cross examination. *Language in Society*, 41(4), 471–97.

(2013). *Aboriginal Ways of Using English*. Canberra: Aboriginal Studies Press.

(2016a). Judicial understandings of Aboriginality and language use. *The Judicial* Review, 12, 471–90.

(2016b). Theorising language in sociolinguistics and the law: (How) can sociolinguistics have an impact on inequality in the criminal justice process? In N. Coupland, ed., *Sociolinguistics: Theoretical Debates*. Cambridge: Cambridge University Press, pp. 367–89.

(2018). Communicating the right to silence to Aboriginal suspects: Lessons from Western Australia v Gibson. *Journal of Judicial Administration*, 28, 4–21.

Eades, D., & Arends, J. (2004). (eds.). Special section: Language analysis and determination of nationality. *International Journal of Speech, Language and the Law* 11(2), 179–266.

Eades, D., Fraser, H., Siegel, J., McNamara, T., & Baker, B. (2003). Linguistic identification in the determination of nationality: A preliminary report. *Language Policy*, 2(2), 179–99.

Eades, D., & Pavlenko A. (2016). Translating research into policy: New guidelines for communicating rights to non-native speakers. *Language and Law/Linguagem e Direito*, 3(2), 45–64.

Eagleson, R. (1990). *Writing in Plain English*. Canberra: Australian Government.

(1994). Forensic analysis of written personal texts: A case study. In Gibbons, ed., pp. 362–73.

Ehrlich, S. (2012). Text trajectories, legal discourse and gendered inequalities. *Applied Linguistics Review*, 3, 47–73.

Ehrlich, S., & Eades, D. (2016). Introduction: Linguistic and discursive dimensions of consent. In Ehrlich, Eades & Ainsworth, eds., pp. 1–20.

Ehrlich, S., Eades, D., & Ainsworth, J., eds. (2016) *Discursive Constructions of Consent in the Legal Process*. Oxford: Oxford University Press.

Evans, N. (2002). Country and the Word: Linguistic evidence in the Croker sea claim. In J. Henderson & D. Nash, eds., *Language in Native Title*. Canberra: Australian Institute of Aboriginal and Torres Strait Islander Studies, pp. 53–100.

Findling, J., & Heydon, G. (2016) Questioning the evidence: A case for best-practice models of interviewing in the Refugee Review Tribunal. *Journal of Judicial Administration*, 26(4), 19–30.

Ford, W. K., & Mertz, E. (2016). Introduction: Translating law and social science. In Mertz, Ford & Matoesian, eds., pp. 1–26.

Fraser, H. (2009). The role of 'educated native speakers' in providing language analysis for the determination of the origin of asylum seekers. *International Journal of Speech Language and the Law*, *16*(1), 113–38.

(2011). The role of linguists and native speakers in language analysis for the determination of speaker origin: A response to Tina Cambier-Langeveld. *International Journal of Speech Language and the Law*, 18(1), 121–30.

(2012). Bayes and beyond: The complex challenges of LADO and their relevance to forensic speaker comparison. In C. Donohue, S. Ishihara, & W. Steed, eds., *Quantitative Approaches to Problems in Linguistics: Studies in Honour of Phil Rose*. Munich: LINCOM Europa, pp. 215–22.

(2013). Covert recordings as evidence in court: The return of police 'verbal-ling'? *The Conversation*. https://theconversation.com/covert-recordings-as-evidence-in-court-the-return-of-police-verballing-14072.

(2018). Forensic transcription: How confident false beliefs about language and speech threaten the right to a fair trial in Australia. *Australian Journal of Linguistics*, *38*(4), 586–606.

(2019). The role of native speakers in LADO: Are we missing a more important question? In Patrick, Schmid & Zwaan (eds)., pp. 71–89.

(2020a). Introducing the research hub for language in forensic evidence. *Judicial Officers' Bulletin*, 32(11), 117–8.

(2020b). Forensic transcription: The case for transcription as a dedicated area of linguistic science. In Coulthard, May, & Sousa-Silva, eds., pp. 416–31.

(2021). The development of legal procedures for using a transcript to assist the jury in understanding indistinct covert recordings used as evidence in Australian criminal trials: A history in three key cases. *Language and Law / Linguagem e Direito*, 8(1), 59–75.

(2022a). A framework for deciding how to create and evaluate transcripts for forensic and other purposes. *Frontiers in Communication*, 7, 898410.

(2022b). Forensic transcription: Legal and scientific perspectives. In C. Bernardasci, D. Dipino, D. Garassino et al., eds., *Speaker Individuality in Phonetics and Speech Sciences: Speech Technology and Forensic Applications*. Milano: Officinaventuno, pp. 19–32.

Fraser, H., & Kinoshita, Y. (2021). Injustice arising from the unnoticed power of priming: How lawyers and even judges can be misled by unreliable transcripts of indistinct forensic audio. *Criminal Law Journal*, 45(3), 142–52.

Fraser, H., & Loakes, D. (2020). Acoustic injustice: The experience of listening to indistinct covert recordings presented as evidence in court. *Law Text Culture*, 24, 405–29.

Fraser, H., & Stevenson, B. (2014). The power and persistence of contextual priming: More risks in using police transcripts to aid jurors' perception of poor quality covert recordings. *The International Journal of Evidence and Proof*, 18(3), 205–29.

Freckelton, I., & Selby, H. (eds.). (2019). *Expert Evidence*, 6th ed., Sydney: Lawbook.

French, P. (2017). Developmental history of forensic speaker comparison in the UK. *English Phonetics*, 16(1), 271–86.

French, P., & Fraser, H. (2018). Why 'ad hoc experts' should not provide transcripts of indistinct forensic audio, and a proposal for a better approach. *Criminal Law Journal*, 42, 298–302.

Fryer-Smith, S. (2008). *Aboriginal Cultural Awareness Benchbook for Western Australian Courts*, 2nd ed., Perth: Australian Institute of Judicial Administration.

Gaykamangu, J. G. (2012). Ngarra law: Aboriginal customary law from Arnhem Land. *Northern Territory Law Journal*, 2, 236–48.

Gibbons, J. (1990). Applied linguistics in court. *Applied Linguistics*, 11(3), 229–37.

(ed.). (1994). *Language and the Law*, London: Longman.

(1995). What got lost?: The place of electronic recording and interpreting in police interviews. In Eades, ed., pp. 175–86.

(2001). Revising the language of New South Wales police procedures: Applied Linguistics in action. *Applied Linguistics*, 22(4), 439–69.

(2003). *Forensic Linguistics*. Oxford: Basil Blackwell.

(2017). Towards clearer jury instructions. *Language and Law / Linguagem e Direito*, 4(1), 142–60.

Granhag, P. A., Vrij, A., & Verschuere, B. (2015). *Detecting Deception: Current Challenges and Cognitive Approaches*. Chichester: John Wiley & Sons.

Goddard, C. (1996). Can linguists help judges know what they mean? Linguistic semantics in the courtroom. *Forensic Linguistics*, 3(2), 250-72.

Gray, P. R. A. (2000). Do the walls have ears? Indigenous title and courts in Australia. *International Journal of Legal Information*, 28, 185–211.

(2011). The expert witness problem. *International Journal of Speech, Language and the Law*, 17(2), 201–9.

(2021). Aboriginal claimants: Adjusting legal procedures to accommodate linguistic and cultural issues in hearings in Aboriginal land rights claims in the Northern Territory of Australia. In Coulthard, May & Sousa-Silva, eds., pp. 329–43.

(2022/2023). Gratuitous concurrence: When 'yes' might not mean 'I agree'. *Victorian Bar News*, 172, 81–2.

Grey, A. (2021). *Language Rights in a Changing China: A National Overview and Zhuang Case Study*. Berlin: De Gruyter Mouton.

Grey, A., & Smith-Khan, L. (2021). Bringing linguistic research into legal scholarship and practice. *Alternative Law Journal*, 46(1), 64–70.

Grey, A., & Severin A. (2022). Building towards best practice for governments' public communications in languages other than English: a case study of New South Wales, Australia. *Griffith Law Review*, 31(1), 25–56.

Hale, S. (2004). *The Discourse of Court Interpreting: Discourse Practices of the Law, the Witness and the Interpreter*. Amsterdam: John Benjamins.

(2011). Interpreter Policies, Practices and Protocols in Australian Courts and Tribunals – A National Survey, Australasian Institute of Judicial Administration, Melbourne, 89, www.aija.org.au/online/Pub%20no89.pdf.

(2013). Helping interpreters to truly and faithfully interpret the evidence: The importance of briefing and preparation materials. *Australian Bar Review*, 37, 307–20.

Hale, S., Goodman-Delahunty, J., & Martschuk, N. (2019). Interpreter performance in police interviews: Differences between trained professional interpreters and untrained bilinguals. *The Interpreter and Translator Trainer*, 13(2), 107–131.

Hale, S., Goodman-Delahunty, J., Martschuk, N., & Lim, J. (2022). Does interpreter location make a difference? A study of remote vs face-to-face interpreting in simulated police interviews. *Interpreting: International Journal of Research and Practice in Interpreting*, 24(2), 221–53.

Hale, S., Martschuk, N., Goodman-Delahunty, J., Taibi, M., & Xu, H. (2020). Interpreting profanity in police interviews. *Multilingua*, 39, 369–93.

Hale, S., Martschuk, N., Ozolins, U., & Stern, L. (2017). The effect of interpreting modes on witness credibility assessments. *Interpreting*, 19(1), 69–96.

Hale, S., & Stern, L. (2011). Interpreter quality and working conditions: Comparing Australian and international courts of justice. *Judicial Officers Bulletin*, 23(9), 75–9.

Hale, S., San Roque, M., Spencer, D., & Napier, J. (2017). Deaf citizens as jurors in Australian courts: Participating via professional interpreters. *International Journal of Speech, Language and the Law*, 24(2), 151–76.

Hall, M. C., & Collins, A. M. (1980). The admission of spectrographic evidence: A note on Reg. v. Gilmore. *Australian Law Journal*, 54, 21–4.

Hammarström, G. (1987). Voice Identification. *Australian Journal of Forensic Sciences*, 19(3), 95–9.

Haworth, K. J. (2018). Tapes, transcripts and trials. *International Journal of Evidence and Proof*, 22(4), 428–50.

Heydon, G. (1998). Participation frameworks, discourse features and embedded requests in police V.A.T.E. interviews with children. *Monash University Linguistics Papers*, 1 (2), 21–32.

(2005). *The Language of Police Interviewing*. Hampshire: Palgrave Macmillan.

(2007). When silence means acceptance: Understanding the right to silence as a linguistic phenomenon. *Alternative Law Journal*, 32(3), 147–51.

(2008a). The importance of being (in)formal: Discourse strategies in police interviews with children. In K. Kredens & S. Gozdz-Roszkowski, eds., *Language and the Law: International Outlooks*. Bern: Peter Lang, pp. 279–303.

(2008b). The art of deception: Myths about lie detection in written confessions. In L. Smets & A. Vrij, eds., *Cahiers Police Studies: Het Analyseren van de Geloofwaardigheid van Verhoren: Het Gebruik van Leugendetectiemethoden.* [The analysis of the credibility of interrogations: The use of lie detection methods] Gent: Politeia, pp. 173–86.

(2012). Helping the police with their enquiries: Enhancing the investigative interview with linguistic research. *The Police Journal*, 85(2), 101–22.

(2019). *Researching Forensic Linguistics: Approaches and Applications*. Milton Park: Routledge.

Heydon, G., & Lai, M. (2013). Police interviews mediated by interpreters: An exercise in diminishment? *Investigative Interviewing: Research and Practice*, 5(2), 82–98.

Heydon, G., & Mabasso, E. (2018). How are language challenges in domestic violence reporting understood by justice stakeholders in Mozambique? *Language Matters*, 49 (1), 84–106.

Heydon, G., & Powell, A. (2018) Written response interview protocols: An innovative approach to confidential reporting and victim interviewing in sexual assault investigations. *Policing and Society*, 28(6), 631–46.

Hudson, T., McDougall, K., & Hughes, V. (2021). Forensic phonetics. In R.-A. Knight & J. Setter, eds., *Cambridge Handbook of Phonetics*. Cambridge: Cambridge University Press, pp. 631–56.

Ingram, J., Prandolini, R., & Ong, S. (1996). Formant trajectories as indices of phonetic variation for speaker identification. *International Journal of Speech, Language and the Law*, 3(1), 129–45.

Ishihara, S. (2014). A likelihood ratio-based evaluation of strength of authorship attribution evidence in SMS messages using N-grams. *International Journal of Speech, Language and the Law*, 21(1), 23–49.

(2017). Strength of forensic text comparison evidence from stylometric features: A multivariate likelihood ratio-based analysis. *International Journal of Speech, Language and the Law*, 24(1), 67–98.

Jensen, M.-T. (1995). Linguistic evidence accepted in the case of a non-native speaker of English. In Eades, ed., pp. 127–46.

Jones, A. (1994). The limitations of voice identification. In Gibbons, ed., pp. 346–61.

Judicial Commission of New South Wales. (2022). 21st update, *Equality before the Law Benchbook*. Sydney: Judicial Commission of New South Wales.

Judicial Council on Cultural Diversity (JCCD). (2022). Recommended National Standards for Interpreting in Courts and Tribunals, 2nd ed., https://jccd .org.au/publications/.

Kinoshita, Y., & Ishihara, S. (2015). Background population: How does it affect LR based forensic voice comparison? *International Journal of Speech Language and the Law*, 21(2), 191–224.

Koch, H. (1985). Nonstandard English in an Aboriginal land claim. In J. Pride, ed., *Cross-cultural Encounters: Communication and Miscommunication*. Melbourne: River Seine Publications, pp. 176–95.

Koehler, J. J. (2013). Linguistic confusion in court: Evidence from the forensic sciences. *Journal of Law and Policy*, 21(2), 515–39.

Kreiman, J. & Sidtis, D. (2011). *Foundations of Voice Studies: An Interdisciplinary Approach to Voice Production and Perception*. Oxford: Wiley Blackwell.

La Rooy, D., Heydon, G., Korkman, J., & Myklebust, T. (2015). Interviewing child witnesses. In G. Oxburgh, T. Myklebust, T. Grant & R. Milne, eds., *Communication in Investigative and Legal contexts: Integrated Approaches from Forensic Psychology, Linguistics and Law Enforcement*. Chichester: John Wiley & Sons, pp. 57–78.

Lai, M., & Mulayim, S. (2014). Interpreter linguistic intervention in the strategies employed by police in investigative interviews. *Police Practice and Research*, 15(4), 307–21.

Lakoff, G., & Johnson, M. H. (1980). *Metaphors We Live By*. Chicago: University of Chicago Press.

Langford, I. (2000). Forensic semantics: The meaning of *murder, manslaughter* and *homicide*. *Forensic Linguistics*, 7(1), 72–94.

Language and National Origin Group (2004). Guidelines for the use of language analysis in relation to questions of national origin in refugee cases. *International Journal of Speech, Language and the Law*, 11(2), 261–66.

Law Society of South Australia (2020). Lawyers' Protocols for Dealing with Aboriginal Clients in South Australia. www.lawsocietysa.asn.au/Public/ Publications/Resources_Hub.aspx.

Law Society of the Northern Territory (2015). *Indigenous Protocols for Lawyers in the Northern Territory*, 2nd ed. Darwin. Law Society Northern Territory. www.lawsocnt.asn.au/fmi/xsl/lsnt/lsnt_publications.xsl.

Lee, J. (2009). Interpreting inexplicit language during courtroom examination. *Applied Linguistics*, 30(1), 93–114.

Liddicoat, A., & Haugh, M. (eds.). (2009). *Conceptualising Communication*. Special issue of *Australian Journal of Linguistics* 29(1).

Lo Bianco, J. (1987). *National Policy on Languages*. Canberra: Australian Government.

Loakes, D. (2008). A forensic phonetic investigation into the speech patterns of identical and non-identical twins. *International Journal of Speech Language and the Law*, 15(1), 97–100.

Loakes, D., & McDougall, K. (2010). Individual variation in the frication of voiceless plosives in Australian English: A study of twins. *Australian Journal of Linguistics*, 30(2), 155–81.

Loakes, D., Clothier, J., Hajek, J., & Fletcher, J. (2014). An investigation of the /el/–/æl/ merger in Australian English: A pilot study on production and perception in South-West Victoria. *Australian Journal of Linguistics*, 34 (4), 436–52.

Loney-Howes, R., & Heydon, G. (2018). Reporting sexual assault anonymously: an analysis of the Sexual Assault Reporting Anonymous (SARA) mobile application and website: 2013-2016. South Eastern Centre Against Sexual Assault (unpublished).

Loney-Howes, R., Heydon, G., & O'Neill, T. (2021). Connecting survivors to therapeutic support and criminal justice through informal reporting options: An analysis of sexual violence reports made to a digital reporting tool in Australia. *Current Issues in Criminal Justice*, 34 (1), 20–37.

Luchjenbroers, J. (1997). 'In your own words...': Questions and answers in a Supreme Court trial. *Journal of Pragmatics*, 27, 477–503.

Mabasso, E. (2019). Tell us the story in your Portuguese: We can understand you. In M. Ralarala, R. Kaschula & G. Heydon, eds., *New Frontiers in Forensic Linguistics: Themes and Perspectives in Language and Law in Africa and Beyond*. Stellenbosch: African Sun Press, pp. 33–48.

MacFarlane, J., Kurt, C., Heydon, G., & Roh, A. (2019) 'Like giving a wheelchair to someone who should be walking': Interpreter access and the problematisation of linguistic diversity in the justice system. In M. Ralarala, R. Kaschula & G. Heydon, eds., *New Frontiers in Forensic Linguistics*. Stellenbosch: African Sun Press pp. 51–70.

Markham, D. (1999). Listeners and disguised voices: The imitation and perception of dialectal accent. *International Journal of Speech Language and the Law*, 6(2), 290–99.

Maley, Y. (1994). The language of the law. In Gibbons, ed., pp. 11–50.

(2000). The case of the long-nosed potoroo: The framing and construction of expert witness testimony. In S. Sarangi & M. Coulthard, eds., *Discourse and Social Life*. Essex: Pearson Education, pp. 246–69.

Matoesian, G. (2001). *Law and the Language of Identity: Discourse in the William Kennedy Smith Rape Trial*. Oxford: Oxford University Press.

(2016). Translating token instances of "this" into type patterns of "that": The discursive and multimodal translation of evidence into precedent. In Mertz, Ford & Matoesian, eds., pp. 55–84.

McGorrery, P. G., & McMahon, M. (2016). A fair 'hearing': Earwitness identifications and voice identification parades. *International Journal of Evidence and Proof*, 21(3), 262–86.

McKay, G. (1985). Language issues in training programs for Northern Territory police: A linguist's view. *Australian Review of Applied Linguistics, Series S*, 2, 32–43.

Mertz, E., Ford, W. K., & Matoesian, G. (eds.). (2016), *Translating the Social World for Law: Linguistic Tools for a New Realism*. Oxford: Oxford University Press,

Methven, E. (2018). A little respect: Swearing, police and criminal justice discourse. *International Journal for Crime, Justice and Social Democracy*, 7(3), 58–74.

Mildren, D. (1997). Redressing the imbalance: Aboriginals in the criminal justice system. *Criminal Law Journal*, 21(1), 7–22.

(1999). Redressing the imbalance: Aboriginal people in the criminal justice system. *Forensic Linguistics*, 6(1), 137–60.

(2012). Indigenous Australians and the criminal justice system. *Paper Presented to the Uluru Criminal Lawyers Conference*, August. https://supremecourt.nt.gov.au/__data/assets/pdf_file/0011/727067/indigenous-australians-and-the-criminal-justice-system-criminal-law-conference-uluru.pdf

Milne, B. & Bull, R. (1999). *Investigative Interviewing: Psychology and Practice*. Hoboken, NJ: Wiley-Blackwell.

Moore, D. (2022). Closing the gap in legal communication: The challenges of interpreting Indigenous languages in Central Australian courts. In J. Wakabayashi & M. O'Hagan, eds., *Translating and Interpreting in Australia and New Zealand: Distance and Diversity*. Abingdon: Routledge, pp. 23–43.

Morphy, F. (2007). Performing law: The Yolgnu of Blue Mud Bay meet the native title process. In B. Smith & F. Morphy, eds., *The Social Effects of Native Title: Recognition, Translation, Coexistence*. Canberra: ANU E Press, pp. 31–57.

Morrison, G. S., Enzinger, E., Hughes, V., et al. (2021). Consensus on validation of forensic voice comparison. *Science & Justice*, 61(3), 299–309.

Mulayim, S., Lai, M., & Norma, C. (2015). *Police Investigative Interviews and Interpreting: Context, Challenges, and Strategies*. Boca Raton: CRC Press.

Muniroh, D., Findling, J., & Heydon, G. (2018). What's in a question: A case for a culturally appropriate interviewing protocol in the Australian Refugee Review Tribunal. In I. Nick, ed., *Immigrants, Refugees, Asylum-Seekers, and Forensic Linguistics*. Delaware, USA: Vernon Press, pp. 133–54.

Muniroh, R., & Heydon, G. (2022). Addressing the gap between principles and practices in police interviewing in Indonesia. *Journal of Police and Criminal Psychology*, 37(2), 312–24.

Nakane, I. (2007). Problems in communicating the suspect's rights in interpreted police interviews. *Applied Linguistics*, 28(1), 87–112.

(2014). *Interpreter Mediated Police Interviews: A Discourse-Pragmatic Approach*. Basingstoke: Palgrave Macmillan.

(2020). Courtroom discourse of the 'hybrid' Japanese criminal justice system. *Journal of Asian Linguistic Anthropology*, 1(1), 110–35.

Napier J., Spencer, D., Hale, S., et al. (2019). Changing the international justice landscape: Perspectives on deaf citizenship and jury service. *Sign Language Studies*, 19(2), 240–66.

Napier, J., Spencer, D. & Sabolcec, J. (2007). *Deaf Juror's Access to Court Proceedings via Sign Language Interpreting: An Investigation*, NSW Law Reform Commission Research Report No 14.

Nash, D. (1979). Foreigners in their own land: Aborigines in court. *Legal Service Bulletin*, 4(3), 105–7.

New South Wales Legislative Council Standing Committee on Law and Justice Inquiry. (2014). *Family Response to the Murders in Bowraville*. Report 55. www.parliament.nsw.gov.au/lcdocs/inquiries/2131/Bowraville%20-%20Final%20report.pdf

Nolan, F. (1983). *The Phonetic Bases of Speaker Recognition*. Cambridge, MA: Cambridge University Press.

Olson, D. R. (1994). *The World on Paper: The Conceptual and Cognitive Implications of Writing and Reading*. Cambridge, MA: Cambridge University Press.

Patrick, P. L., Schmid, M. S., & Zwaan, K. (eds.). (2019). *Language Analysis for the Determination of Origin: Current Perspectives and New Directions.* Cham, Switzerland: Springer.

Porter, S., & Ten Brinke, L. (2009). Dangerous decisions: A theoretical framework for understanding how judges assess credibility in the courtroom. *Legal and Criminological Psychology*, 14(1), 119–34.

Queensland Supreme Court (2016). *Equal Treatment Benchbook*, 2nd ed., www.courts.qld.gov.au/court-users/practitioners/benchbooks.

Ralarala, M. K. (2016). An analysis of critical 'voices' and 'styles' in transpreters' translations of complainants' narratives. *Translation and Translanguaging in Multilingual Contexts*, 2(1), 142–66.

Remedy Australia (2021). Advancing jury inclusivity in Australia. www.rem edy.org.au/reports/RemedyAustralia_on_inclusive_juries_2021.pdf.

Robertson, B., Vignaux, G., & Berger, C. (2016). *Interpreting Evidence: Evaluating Forensic Science in the Courtroom.* Chichester: Wiley.

Rock, F. (2007). *Communicating Rights: The Language of Arrest and Detention.* Houndmills: Palgrave Macmillan.

Rose, P. (2002). *Forensic Speaker Identification.* London: Taylor and Francis.

(2013). Where the science ends and the law begins: Likelihood ratio-based forensic voice comparison in a $150 million telephone fraud. *International Journal of Speech Language and the Law*, 20(2), 275–322.

Rose, P., & Duncan, S. (1995). Naive auditory identification and discrimination of similar voices by familiar listeners. *International Journal of Speech Language and the Law*, 2(1), 1–17.

Rose, P., & Morrison, G. (2009). A response to the UK position statement on forensic speaker comparison. *International Journal of Speech Language and the Law*, 16(1), 139–63.

Rusho, D. (2021). Cross-currents: Indigenous language interpreting in Australia's justice system. *International Journal of Speech Language and the Law*, 28(2), 281–8.

Smith-Khan, L. (2017). Different in the same way?: Language, diversity and refugee credibility. *International Journal of Refugee Law*, 29(3), 389–416.

(2019a). Communicative resources and credibility in public discourse on refugees. *Language in Society*, 48(3), 403–27.

(2019b). Why refugee visa credibility assessments lack credibility: A critical discourse analysis. *Griffith Law Review*, 28(4), 406–30.

(2022). Incorporating sociolinguistic perspectives in Australian refugee credibility assessments: The case of CRL18. *Journal of International Migration and Integration*, https://doi.org/10.1007/s12134-022-00937-2.

Snow, P. C., & Powell, M. B. (2005). What's the story? An exploration of narrative language abilities in male juvenile offenders. *Psychology, Crime & Law*, 11(3), 239–53.

Solan, L. (1998). Linguistic experts as semantic tour guides. *Forensic Linguistics*, 5(2), 87–106.

Stern, L. (2001). At the junction of cultures - Interpreting at the international criminal tribunal for the former Yugoslavia in the light of other international interpreting practices. *Judicial Review*, 5(3), 255–74.

Stroud, N. (2010). The Koori Court revisited: Review of cultural and language awareness in the administration of justice. *Australian Law Librarian*, 18 (3), 184–92.

Svartvik, J. (1968). *The Evans Statements, A Case for Forensic Linguistics*. Göteborg: University of Göteborg.

Tiersma, P. (2000). The rocky road to legal reform: Improving the language of jury instructions. *Brooklyn Law Review*, 66, 1081–119.

Tresize, P. (1996). Use of language and the Anunga rules. *Aboriginal Law Bulletin*, 3(79), 17–8.

Trinch, S. (2003). *Latinas' Narratives of Domestic Abuse: Discrepant Versions of Violence*. Amsterdam: John Benjamins.

Victorian Law Reform Commission. (2017). *Plain English and the Law*, 2nd ed., Melbourne: Victorian Law Reform Commission.

Walsh, M. (1994). Interactional styles in the courtroom: An example from northern Australia. In Gibbons, ed., pp. 217–33.

   (1995). Tainted evidence: Literacy and traditional knowledge in an Aboriginal land claim. In Eades, ed., pp. 97–124.

   (2008). 'Which way?' Difficult options for vulnerable witnesses in Australian Aboriginal land claim and native title cases. *Journal of English Linguistics*, 36(3), 239–65.

Wierzbicka, A. (2003). Reasonable man and Reasonable doubt: The English language, Anglo culture and Anglo-American law. *Forensic Linguistics*, 10(1), 1–22.

Zappavigna, M., Dwyer, P., & Martin, J. R. (2016). Consent and compliance in youth justice conferences. In Ehrlich, Eades & Ainsworth, eds., pp. 186–212.

Zappavigna, M., & Martin, J. R. (2018). *Discourse and Diversionary Justice: An Analysis of Youth Justice Conferencing*. Cham, Switzerland: Palgrave Macmillan.

Zwaan, K., Muysken, P., & Verrips, M. (eds.). (2010). *Language and Origin: The Role of Language in European Asylum Procedures: Linguistic and Legal Perspectives*. Nijmegen: Wolf Legal Publishers.

Acknowledgements

Our thanks go to colleagues who thoughtfully read and commented on extracts from the draft, and answered our queries: Alex Bowen, Kate Burridge, Felicity Cox, Michael Cooke, David Deterding, Debbie Loakes, John Gibbons, Peter Gray, John Hajek, Sandra Hale, Helen Harper, Shunichi Ishihara, Yuko Kinoshita, David Moore, Ikuko Nakane, Pam Peters, Phil Rose and Laura Smith-Khan.

In addition, Helen Fraser gratefully acknowledges the generous sharing of historical memories by the following people, without whose help Section 3.2 would not have been possible: Heather Bowe-Dennis, John Ingram, Alex Jones, Duncan Markham, Kirsty McDougall, Hugh Selby, Laura Tollfree.

All remaining errors are the responsibility of the authors.

Cambridge Elements ≡

Forensic Linguistics

Tim Grant

Aston University

Tim Grant is Professor of Forensic Linguistics, Director of the Aston Institute for Forensic Linguistics, and past president of the International Association of Forensic Linguists. His recent publications have focussed on online sexual abuse conversations including *Language and Online Identities: The Undercover Policing of Internet Sexual Crime* (with Nicci MacLeod, Cambridge, 2020).

Tim is one of the world's most experienced forensic linguistic practitioners and his case work has involved the analysis of abusive and threatening communications in many different contexts including investigations into sexual assault, stalking, murder, and terrorism. He also makes regular media contributions including presenting police appeals such as for the BBC *Crimewatch* programme.

Tammy Gales

Hofstra University

Tammy Gales is an Associate Professor of Linguistics and the Director of Research at the Institute for Forensic Linguistics, Threat Assessment, and Strategic Analysis at Hofstra University, New York. She has served on the Executive Committee for the International Association of Forensic Linguists (IAFL), is on the editorial board for the peer-reviewed journals *Applied Corpus Linguistics and Language* and *Law / Linguagem e Direito*, and is a member of the advisory board for the BYU Law and Corpus Linguistics group. Her research interests cross the boundaries of forensic linguistics and language and the law, with a primary focus on threatening communications. She has trained law enforcement agents from agencies across Canada and the U.S. and has applied her work to both criminal and civil cases.

About the Series

Elements in Forensic Linguistics provides high-quality accessible writing, bringing cutting-edge forensic linguistics to students and researchers as well as to practitioners in law enforcement and law. Elements in the series range from descriptive linguistics work, documenting a full range of legal and forensic texts and contexts; empirical findings and methodological developments to enhance research, investigative advice, and evidence for courts; and explorations into the theoretical and ethical foundations of research and practice in forensic linguistics.

Cambridge Elements $\equiv$

Forensic Linguistics

Elements in the Series

The Idea of Progress in Forensic Authorship Analysis
Tim Grant

Forensic Linguistics in the Philippines: Origins, Developments, and Directions
Marilu Rañosa-Madrunio and Isabel Pefianco Martin

The Language of Fake News
Jack Grieve and Helena Woodfield

A Theory of Linguistic Individuality for Authorship Analysis
Andrea Nini

Forensic Linguistics in Australia: Origins, Progress and Prospects
Diana Eades, Helen Fraser and Georgina Heydon